Praise for Molly Fletcher and *Fearless at Work*

"Is fear holding you back from attaining cherished goals, drawing nearer to others, or being the best you can be? Molly Fletcher offers a guide to moving past your fear and trading habitual mindsets for new ways of thinking. This could be your year to be fearless at work—and in life!"

—Daniel H. Pink, *New York Times* bestselling author of *To Sell Is Human* and *Drive*

"If you're ready to turn your dreams into reality, then *Fearless at Work* is the perfect blueprint. Bravo to Molly Fletcher! You are most definitely a Leader Worth Following!"

—Duane Cummings, CEO of Leadercast

"Like many, I have battled fear in life and work—and found that the only effective antidote is to make a daily shift in my thinking from anxiety to anticipation. This book will help you make that transition, which is vital to success."

—Cheryl A. Bachelder, CEO of Popeyes Louisiana Kitchen, Inc., and author of *Dare to Serve*

"Looking to make changes in your professional life? *Fearless at Work* is a book you will turn to again and again for life-changing advice."

—Carol Tome, CFO and EVP Corporate Services at The Home Depot

"A must-read. Molly Fletcher brings to life our choice: whether to live constrained by fear or to push beyond it. This book will teach you how to shift toxic thinking and trade old habits for a new mindset."

—Jim Loehr, EdD,
cofounder of the Johnson & Johnson
Human Performance Institute

"Molly Fletcher provides a fearless road map to help you navigate the fears and pitfalls that too often sabotage our success. Filled with lessons from some of the best and brightest leaders, *Fearless at Work* teaches us how to reframe our thinking and push through the fears that have been holding us back."

—Alison Levine,
New York Times bestselling author of *On the Edge*
and executive producer of *The Glass Ceiling*

FEARLESS
AT WORK

FEARLESS AT WORK

ACHIEVE YOUR POTENTIAL BY TRANSFORMING SMALL MOMENTS INTO BIG OUTCOMES

MOLLY FLETCHER

Mc
Graw
Hill
Education

NEW YORK   CHICAGO   SAN FRANCISCO   ATHENS
LONDON   MADRID   MEXICO CITY   MILAN
NEW DELHI   SINGAPORE   SYDNEY   TORONTO

To Jack —

Be Fearless!

Molly Fletcher

1 2 3 4 5 6 7 8 9   LCR   22 21 20 19 18 17

ISBN 978-1-259-86298-4
MHID   1-259-86298-4

e-ISBN 978-1-259-86299-1
e-MHID   1-259-86299-2

Book design by Lee Fukui and Mauna Eichner

To those with big dreams and aspirations—
here's to living more fearlessly . . . one step at a time

CONTENTS

ACKNOWLEDGMENTS

My gratitude goes out to the people and places that have taught me to embrace the small moments in life—who have taught me to recognize them, embrace them, and, whenever possible, work to turn them into big outcomes.

Thank you to my immediate and extended family. Our connection and love fill us all daily. Thank you for modeling fearless living for me.

Thank you, Sprague Paynter and Tiffany Allen. You are always eager to help and support our mission to inspire, lead, and connect. Thank you.

Thank you, Michelle Hiskey, a brilliant writer whom I am truly honored to have collaborated with in the writing of this book. We have had many small moments together that created big outcomes. I am humbled to have you as a partner on this project. Thank you.

Thank you to my agent, John Willig. You always shoot straight with me, and I love it. Thank you.

Thank you to my editor at McGraw-Hill, Casey Ebro, for your guidance and support. You embraced the small moments of my ideas and helped bring them to life in this final and fabulous product—a book. Thank you, Casey.

Thank you to all the people and places that create the moments (even those that elicit fear). May they continue to do so for all of us. Let us always be thankful for each of them.

FEARLESS AT WORK

INTRODUCTION

Our lives turn on small moments of fearlessness that carry powerful consequences. Too often we are on the sidelines as they unfold. We're not prepared because fear keeps us from acting, or it makes us act to preserve what we know, even if we don't like or want the status quo. Or we're not paying attention.

There are 1,440 minutes in a day. This book is about recognizing those 1,440 moments in your life every day and preparing yourself to act with less fear and more intention. More authenticity. Especially if the life you want is not the one you are living right now.

Fear is real, and it is powerful. But it doesn't have to rule us.

Here's what I wholeheartedly believe when it comes to fear: by practicing acts of fearlessness in the small moments of daily life, we prepare ourselves for big outcomes.

You're probably reading this book because you want something more out of your life—either personally or professionally—and you sense that fear is holding you back. Perhaps you're one of the many people I hear from each day, through one-on-one conversations, e-mails, and letters, who aren't engaged in their work. Recent Gallup research has found that two out of every three workers do not feel involved with, engaged in, or committed to their work.[1]

You want to know right now how to tap more of your energy and potential—if you could get past the fear. You're open to change, but you want specific, clear ways to achieve change that lasts. You want to better speak your truth and act on it in the moment.

So let's do this, through learning to recognize the small moments to practice fearlessness. This is how you will get to the "more" in your life.

———

AS A SPORTS AGENT who reinvented myself as an entrepreneur, consultant, corporate speaker, and author, I intentionally studied and practiced fearlessness.

For two decades, I represented elite athletes, coaches, and broadcasters whose success depended on peak performance. They had learned to navigate fear and create a culture in which others did the same.

Agents specialize in moments.

I worked in a tight gap between where elite performers shine and where they want to—or could—go next. Time may be the biggest factor. For the top athletes, the window to excel is very short, and seizing that moment means everything.

Fear is there, too, believe me. The next time you read about a multi-million-dollar deal being inked, know that both sides pushed beyond fear (this might sound ridiculous, but for some, this is a small moment that can come, go, and never return). Fear paralyzes people, and the higher the stakes, the greater the fear. Fear usually enters the picture when a decision is within reach or a deadline is looming. There's so much on the line that it's easy for people to get anxious and defensive.

So while I was observing my clients' methods of being fearless peak performers, I had to be fearless on their behalf when I negotiated contracts and marketing deals that totaled more than $500 million. I had to conquer fears as I negotiated appearances for Hall of Famers, national championship coaches, PGA Tour winners, Cy Young winners, all-stars, and Emmy Award–winning broadcasters.

And I was usually the only woman in the room. That was another driver to becoming fearless. I could not be scared if I wanted to survive, much less thrive.

———

LET'S TALK ABOUT YOU.

Do you fear change? How about conflict? Maybe it's more specific: an upcoming deadline, a job performance review, or a presentation. Maybe you are afraid to ask for help or to confront a colleague or share a new idea. Perhaps you fear the uncertainty of being able to perform in a crisis or to make the decision that is best for your team. You may fear demotion or losing your job, even if that's unlikely to happen. Fear is like a virus that moves within corporate culture, infecting our ability to innovate and make progress as individuals and members of teams. Why do we stay in a job we aren't engaged in? Because we are scared of change? Scared of the unknown? Why do we not allow ourselves to really dream?

Fear causes people to get stuck in unhealthy patterns and places in life. It is often part of what Stanford University psychologist Carol Dweck calls a "fixed mindset."[2]

We default to labeling as a way to control people and outcomes. In general, we avoid challenges, give up easily, see effort as worthless, ignore constructive criticism, and breed the insecurity that leads to feeling threatened by others' success.

The fear-infused, fixed mindset says, "You either have it or you don't," and if you don't, don't bother trying.

———

FEAR IS FUELED by expectations. Expectations that we will perform to a certain level. Expectations that talent will carry us. That it should carry us. This sense of entitlement masks fear and creates limits. This mindset pigeonholes a person by what he or she is good at, and only by that. The expectations from the outside—the status quo—determine what a person can and should do. The status quo helps us feel like we are doing the right thing without figuring it out for ourselves.

Fear blocks growth, period. Fear can grow in the gap between where we are and where we want to be. It's like looking across a canyon to a beautiful resort. All you can see is the drop-off and no way to get there.

Fear creates a world we don't love, with triggers that serve to keep us trapped. Fear keeps us from realizing that there can be more. More energy, more contentment, more joy. Fearlessness is the way to get across that gap, a bridge to the lives we want to have. And the good news is that we *can* cross that canyon. It is possible to move from a fixed mindset to a growth mindset.

Personally, I don't think success, or the best version of ourselves, is as likely without a direct look at the fears that hold us back. If you are one of the majority who fear a tough conversation or hammering out deal points, for example, how empowering would it be to turn your fear into confidence?

"Hello, fear. Thank you for being here," Cheryl Strayed, the author of *Wild*, tells herself. "You're my indication that I'm doing what I need to do."[3]

Fearlessness is learned through a growth mindset. A person with this way of thinking views others' success as a window into lessons and inspiration for even greater personal success, fueled by the power of free will (not expectation).

A growth mindset draws more than 20 million visitors who learn from Khan Academy's online library of free educational videos. Khan's philosophy: "Most people are held back not by their innate ability, but by their mindset. They think intelligence is fixed, but it isn't. Your brain is like a muscle. The more you use it and struggle, the more it grows. New research shows we can take control of our ability to learn. We can all become better learners. We just need to build our brains in the right way."[4]

So fearlessness is a process, not a single passage. It is achieved breath by breath. It's not a question of moving fast or far or perfectly. It is about having the ability to look at your fears squarely, learn to stay there, and find your inner resources that will help you move through fears. Fearlessness is about keeping going.

Notice that *fear* is a noun and a verb. It is active and solid. I believe that it can be made into something else.

How?

By practicing in the small moments.

People who achieve big outcomes often do so one tiny step at a time. For instance, an Everest climber takes one step at a time, and it's not a direct journey to 29,000 feet. Above 18,000 feet, the body begins to break down, so climbers must make a series of up and down treks to acclimate, eat, hydrate, sleep, and regain strength.[5] On the world's highest peaks, paying attention to the present moment is key to survival.

Here's a more down-to-earth example from my own life. My first job in Atlanta was with the Super Bowl Host Committee, the centralized planning entity that managed hundreds of daily requests and inquiries in the year leading up to the big game. I was part of a small team that worked in a big building downtown with no windows, which gives you an idea of my outlook.

The job sounded important, but it sure didn't feel that way. On the one hand, I fielded calls from the NFL commissioner and the chief marketing officers of big brands such as Coca-Cola, Home Depot, and Chick-fil-A. On the other hand, I worked for a supervisor who came in late, communicated zero gratitude and authenticity, and enjoyed keeping callers on hold—a power play. In the middle of these ridiculous office games, I felt afraid that this was all there was for me. Like I had nowhere to go beyond saying hundreds of times a day, "Super Bowl 28, this is Molly."

On days when I was particularly down, especially during short winter days that made me feel like I would never see sunshine again, I would call my parents, crying. Dad would either try to get me to quit and come home to Michigan or tell me about all the jerks he had worked for over the years. Somehow I managed to drag myself back to work the next day.

I particularly hated when VIPs showed up and wasted their time waiting for the supervisor to greet them. I felt like it was my fault they were waiting, and I feared the backlash from them (that I was incompetent for keeping them waiting and not getting them access sooner) and my supervisor (that I was worthless no matter what I did or how hard I tried).

Then I took a hard look at my reality. I asked myself what I was truly afraid of, given that this job would end after the Super Bowl. As I saw more clearly how my fears were ruling me, that reality check opened my eyes to the little opportunities presented by my supervisor's power plays. I could make small talk with the NFL commissioner and other VIPs while they were waiting, either in person or on the phone. Just as important, I was practicing how to conduct business with people who were often annoyed or even hostile.

These opportunities gave me momentum. I developed a help-me-or-hire-me goal and attitude. I connected with everyone, anticipating that they could make a difference in my career, and one day, I might help them as well. After the Super Bowl, I had a sizable list of VIPs I could turn to for advice, and those contacts led me to my career as a sports agent.

———

COMPLEX TASKS OFTEN evoke fear, and to counter that, we need a clear way to focus on what is most important in the moment. "Simple can be harder than complex; you have to work hard to get your thinking clean to make it simple," Apple cofounder Steve Jobs said.

In so many ways, we do better when we break down a big goal into smaller bits. For example, if you want to run a sub-seven-minute mile, you create a timeline and a process to attack this goal daily, shaving seconds off your mile time with each run. Or if a Major League pitcher comes back after arm surgery, he takes little steps each day to get back to or exceed his previous production.

Thinking in small steps helps us think more rationally and less emotionally. It helps us find meaning too. If you have ever lost a friend or family member suddenly, you know that feeling of appreciation for every day and minute. We understand that we have only the present moment of life, and everything else is either a memory or a plan.

We grow by recognizing and valuing incremental progress. The San Antonio Spurs demonstrated this power on their way to winning five NBA titles.[6] Their coach found an inspirational quote from journalist Jacob Riis:

> When nothing seems to help, I go look at a stonecutter
> hammering away at his rock, perhaps a hundred times
> without as much as a crack showing in it. Yet at the hun-
> dred and first blow, it will split in two, and I know it was not
> that blow that did it, but all that had gone before.

These words helped the Spurs find meaning in the daily grind—the workouts, the long season, the injuries, and the constant demands on their physical health, families, and time. Every day they were each striking a blow for their common goal.

The Riis quote also helped create a sense of anticipation: What blow will crack the rock? Will I be ready to step up and deliver? Suspense is part of play. Inspiration keeps drudgery away. When we practice fearlessness, we also protect the sense of joy and fun we experience doing what we love, so our own unique passions never become a grind.

———

THIS BOOK WILL help you pay attention to small opportunities to practice your values, help others, and take a risk to create a new ritual that will push you toward your purpose. Thinking small can lead to taking small steps in a new direction. All those steps make up a journey to big moments—and your highest performance. It's up to you to identify these small moments and seize their potential, especially if you want to make big moves. This is the easiest, most consistent way to become fearless.

I recognize the fear of change, especially the big push that is needed to go from good to great. In 2007, I was representing an all-star stable of professional athletes, coaches, and broadcasters. I was earning a healthy six-figure salary and raising three daughters. It was all that I thought I wanted, including the approval of others. Who would walk away from that?

I did. I felt a purpose calling me for something greater in my life, even if it meant there was no guarantee of success. I knew I could help more people, and my personal and family life could have better balance.

As my children grew, I was reminded of how short life is. The part of me that feared risk and change began to pivot: What if I don't pursue my greater purpose?

It was easy for others to miss the fact that I was changing my life to achieve more control of my time and schedule, more balance, more impact. Many who knew me only superficially wondered: *What is she doing giving up a dream job to go out on her own?* I could see the confusion in the faces of my celebrity clients and fellow sports agents. They were counting on my attention 24/7, and I had spent years giving it to them.

The answer to that dilemma was my obsession with human performance.

As a kid, the idea of success had always captivated me. What separated winners, especially in my sport of tennis? How much was sheer talent, and how much was mental preparation? I watched my mother excel at volunteer leadership in our community and speak effortlessly to large groups and motivate them to take action. I saw myself in a role like hers, leading and inspiring others.

When I became a high school senior, my high school rejected me as commencement speaker, but that didn't dampen my dream. It revived when I became a sports agent and watched my athletes and coaches get paid handsomely for corporate speeches. I began to imagine what I would say to big audiences to help them succeed and to visualize this work allowing me more time with my family.

Would fear of leaving the familiar, and possibly failing, keep me in the familiar? What if my message wouldn't resonate? What if I couldn't make a living from speaking and consulting? What if those fears came true?

It was my turn to say no to fear and yes to fearlessness. It was time to act fearlessly.

From the field of sports representation, I reinvented myself as my own boss in another world where fear is a deal breaker: public speaking.

Speaking in front of others is one of the most common fears in our society, but what I learned about fearless peak performance in sports helps me every time I step on a stage. Companies trust that my message is worth the time of the hundreds or thousands of people in the audience. In that arena, there's no room for fear as I speak to inspire fearlessness in others.

No is a word very familiar to all of us who work in high-pressure environments, who feel that there's something missing, who long for more, who feel the clock ticking.

I write this with the fervent hope that you will gain inspiration and instruction about how to speak up compassionately and take action in the small moments.

Fear can't be eliminated, but we can work through it. You achieve this by *creating awareness of key moments and learning to trade a current behavior for a better one that builds fearlessness*. In this book, I identify dozens of ways you can exchange a fear-based habit for a fearless one.

These trades are small but significant changes to your thinking and actions. Over time, they create a big impact. They will strengthen the positive habits and root out the toxic patterns. Your fear will be replaced by confidence.

- **"Fearless Fundamentals"** (Chapter 1) are five habits that influence all the rest. If you make time to read and apply only these trades, you will be on your way to greater fearlessness.

- **"Anchoring Your Values"** (Chapter 2) will knit your new actions to your deepest beliefs. These five trades are key to identifying small moments in which your authentic self learns to shine without fear.

- **"Maximizing Your Focus"** (Chapter 3) in the small moments through these five trades you practice the concentration and attention of an elite performer so that fearlessness becomes an automatic function.

- **"Stretching Critical Moments"** (Chapter 4) decodes how top performers embrace fear at critical turning points to achieve remarkable feats. They bend time with these four trades, and you can too.

- **"Redirecting Persistent Behaviors"** (Chapter 5) enables you to identify and adapt recurrent habits that you may not even know are working against you to keep you fearful. Change old habits with strong intention. Five trades total.

- **"Reframing Bad News"** (Chapter 6) helps you be prepared for when things go wrong. With these five trades, you will fearlessly embrace and make the most of small moments that you might otherwise miss.

- **"Shifting Toxic Thinking"** (Chapter 7) are five trades that will help you recognize and weed out persistent fear-based thoughts and plant rituals that will drive your best outcomes.

- **"Reprogramming Your Default Settings"** (Chapter 8) examines patterns of thoughts and actions that are so natural, you may not even think of them as fear-based. These five trades represent a reboot for greater fearlessness.

- **"Reinventing Your Perspective"** (Chapter 9) offers five trades to create a formidable new lens of clarity and put the blinders on fear.

- **"Unifying Your Tribe"** (Chapter 10) are three trades that will help you lead fearlessly within your work team, family, or any group—one small moment at a time.

These tools will benefit you by creating awareness and fostering courage to live fearlessly. Through personal anecdotes that are easy to grasp, you will find concrete ways to develop new rituals.

The path to fearlessness is an individual journey, so pick the trades that resonate with you. Put them to work for you immediately.

Two important notes to getting the biggest bang from this book:

1. Get clear on your personal mission. Purpose is everything, and you will notice multiple references to it in this book. My personal mission statement is this: "To connect, inspire, and lead with creative courage and optimism."

Purpose is the rocket programmed to reach your unique destination. Fearlessness is the fuel.

My purpose helped me understand that I needed to leave my work as a sports agent, in part because my success depended on someone else's behavior. That was not enough for me.

My purpose helped me see where I needed to go, what fears stood in my way, and the trades I would need to make to think and act fearlessly. My purpose strengthened my relationships. If there is one regret from my sports agent days, it is that I did not work more with my clients on their own mission statements.

If you don't have a clear purpose, you are more likely to sacrifice your time, energy, and resources to the desires of others and to stay in a place of passivity and fear. I can't say enough about how hard this is, how much commitment it takes, and how satisfying it is to embrace and follow your unique purpose—not to mention how much of an edge it gives you over your competitors who don't want to or can't do this rigorous work.

A strong mission statement that captures your passion and individuality will become an important lens through which to view everything. You will use it to clearly identify the small opportunities to change your behavior and trade for fearlessness. You will be free to say no when everyone around you thinks you should say yes. You will have the vision to surround yourself with a tribe who supports your fearless pursuit of your purpose.

2. Embrace vulnerability. The greatest change happens when we surrender completely. This requires being vulnerable. It takes a great deal of strength to say that your previous way of doing things isn't working anymore. You cannot do this by yourself.

Vulnerability does not mean being weak or submissive. On the contrary, it implies the courage to be yourself. It means "replacing 'professional distance and cool' with uncertainty, risk, and emotional exposure," according to *Harvard Business Review* author Emma Seppala.[7] "Opportunities for vulnerability present themselves to us at work every day. Examples include calling an employee or colleague who lost a deal, reaching out to someone who has just experienced a loss in his or her family, asking someone for help, taking responsibility for something that went wrong at work, or asking your boss or employees what you can do better."

When I visualize vulnerability, I think of the reality show *Dancing with the Stars*. Celebrities compete with professional ballroom dancers, and under harsh spotlights, their every move is critiqued by judges and fans. They are vulnerable, knowing that they can't do it alone.

They depend on their partners to make them look good or at least to keep them from embarrassing themselves. They accept the exposure as a way of showing a different side of themselves. Often they are in the middle of reinventing themselves, and they use the show as a way to tell their new story—that they are more than a former pro athlete, for instance. They aren't afraid to look foolish. They aren't afraid to fail. An attitude of vulnerability is integral to fearlessness.

You demonstrate vulnerability by letting go of perfection and the illusion of power. For many of us, that may involve acknowledging a higher power. Whatever your view of the world, vulnerability will help equip you with new rituals for a life of fearlessness.

You achieve a fearless mindset when you trade your typical reactions and habits for new ways of thinking and acting that position you for your greatest success and fulfillment.

This book comes with a promise: by adopting these small changes, over time, you will begin to see your life change. You will be more aware and motivated. You will make better decisions aligned with your true values. Tough conversations will become easier and even welcome. You will unleash your best energy.

One moment at a time, you will become fearless.

FEARLESS FUNDAMENTALS

It's your place in the world; it's your life.
Go on and do all you can with it,
and make it the life you want to live.
—Mae Jemison, first African-American
woman astronaut

We are all in the middle of something right now. But are we thinking about now? Or are we stuck in the past or future?

The past says: *If only I had . . .*

The future says: *Someday I will . . .*

And that kind of thinking allows fear to take hold.

Fearlessness stays present, and that's what these fundamental habits are about. The here and now.

By recognizing the moment that you are in and its potential, you can begin to create profound changes in the way you think and act.

These five trades will give you insights into how to make small changes in your thinking and behavior and achieve more success and fulfillment.

Now is always between *past* and *present*. *Now* is the middle. The middle is where most of us are functioning in our work life, too.

As a speaker, I am the go-between, carrying a message to a specific audience. As an agent, I made my living in the middle—most of us do.

An agent is anyone who acts on behalf of something or someone else. A good agent doesn't wait for something to happen but rather causes something to happen.

Fearless Fundamentals will help you begin to see yourself as the agent of your life, your goals, and your highest purpose.

There is more out there for you right now. Let's start moving toward it—fearlessly.

Trade Defensiveness for Curiosity

"Be curious and honest, and keep an open heart. Great things will happen." Radio producer Dave Isay wrote these wise words after years of recording and listening to small memories. Taken together, these moments have achieved a massive outcome.[1]

Isay's project—StoryCorps—has created a vast archive of oral histories collected by family members and friends. Today more than 50,000 interviews with 100,000 participants are preserved in the Library of Congress.

This was possible only because Isay overcame a big obstacle. Everyday Americans didn't always realize their life stories were worth documenting and sharing with strangers. They didn't think what they had lived through was that interesting or important to anyone else, even their families.

If you don't see the worth of doing something that forces you out of your comfort zone, it's easy to stay in your shell. To keep your story to yourself. To not venture out of your own perspective. This defensiveness had kept many people from communicating their important life lessons.

Isay broke this ice by starting with two simple words of fearlessness: *What if?*

What if strangers could find common ground by telling their stories?

His curiosity ultimately inspired people to overcome their reluctance to talk. Families confronted their secrets. Estranged friends reconciled. StoryCorps audiences learned to care about strangers and the groups they represented.[2] Isay's vision earned a MacArthur Genius Fellowship.

Curiosity can help you achieve what has never been done. It's a remarkable tool for weeding out a major obstacle to growth: defensiveness.

Defensiveness is the flip side of wanting approval. And approval can keep us under the control of others' opinions and feedback.

Curiosity is so important for leaders.[3] Without curiosity, Home Depot's existence, and success, could not have happened.

Arthur Blank and Bernie Marcus had every reason to be defensive. When the hardware chain they worked for was bought out, they thought they were too valuable to be fired. They were wrong.

But instead of getting defensive, they got busy testing an idea. They had been curious about whether a discount warehouse for do-it-yourselfers would take off. So they put together a proposal, and an investment firm liked the idea and bankrolled it. The Home Depot would thrive, the men thought, by providing solutions for homeowners in all their home improvement projects.

On opening weekend, Blank and Marcus were eager to see how their marketing gimmick would work. Kids would hand out dollar bills as thank-yous to people coming into their new stores. That idea, and the opening of their first two stores, bombed. "We just sat there in stunned silence," Marcus remembered. "It looked like curtains for us. My wife wouldn't let me shave for days. She didn't want me to have a razor in my hands."[4]

But their idea soon was validated by word of mouth, and the cofounders stayed curious. They would regularly pop into Home Depot stores unannounced to see from the sales floor what the merchandising issues were and what the customers were seeking. "A learning experience and an opportunity to change," Blank called it in his autobiography, *Built from Scratch*.

A multi-billion-dollar business was born because Blank and Marcus refused to get stuck in defensiveness after getting fired. By becoming curious, they took their focus off past misfortunes and committed themselves to possibilities.

Defensiveness doesn't help anyone move to a better place in life. It communicates that you don't want or need support. You're telling people you'd rather go on without them.

When I made my career transition, I couldn't afford to be defensive, although there were many times I could have drawn those shades, believe me.

My public speaking work began slowly. I accepted opportunities to speak for free to college groups and other small gatherings. When a friend agreed to help me get started in corporate speaking, I knew that my lack of name recognition could keep me from reaching my goal of being among the top tier of speakers. I realized that I needed to execute a great speech every time, to go well above the bar of expectations. And I wanted to measure this.

I began to distribute surveys to my audiences, asking for ratings and feedback. My goal was to get ratings in the 9s and 10s. Anything less than that attracted my curiosity.

In the small but critical moments, I studied my less stellar report cards for clues to what I could do better: What value could I add to make each keynote a home run? How could I connect and make an impact on each and every person in the room?

As I incorporated these responses into my work little by little, several big things happened. I got better at speaking and delivering more than what my clients expected, from the stage and providing support after events. This led me to higher tiers in this new world, which translated into making a bigger impact both at home and at work.

Most important, trading defensiveness for curiosity made me feel bulletproof. Criticism didn't make me feel victimized. In fact, accepting it with an open mind was part of a strategy to be the best I could be. Letting go of defensiveness gave me more room for positive energy and growth.

Curiosity reframes the conversation. It takes feedback and criticism and embraces it as fuel for growth. No matter what work you are in, your success depends on your being bigger than the problems you seek to address.

Be aware the next time you feel your hackles going up. Experiment with a new response. Instead of getting defensive, can you ask a question to elicit more information? Can you ask, "What if?"

Because defensiveness is so natural, trading it for curiosity—as hard as that is—immediately creates results. If you don't believe me, just ask Dave Isay, Bernie Marcus, and Arthur Blank!

Trade the Old Story for a New Story

Fear is a story we tell ourselves.

Dan Jansen, the Olympic speed skater, famously overcame repeated Olympic heartbreak to capture gold in his final race. Jansen worked with Dr. Jim Loehr, a friend of mine and a prominent sports psychologist and bestselling author who has helped elite athletes overcome the mental barriers inhibiting their performance. Jansen set a goal while working with Loehr to break the 36-second barrier in the 500 meters. At the time, it was thought to be physically impossible, and when people buy into a story like that, it becomes a self-limiting belief.

But Jansen rescripted the truth. He wrote, as Loehr told him to, the number "35.99" in his training log every single day. This ritual led him to expect to break 36 seconds. Jansen wrote his own story and became the first person to break the barrier. After he broke the mark, the barrier crumbled, and multiple others did within the next year.

These moments helped set up Jansen for rewriting a much bigger story. Beginning with the 1988 Calgary Games, when he was unnerved by the death of his sister, Jansen had failed to win an Olympic medal in 1992 and in his 500-meter specialty in 1994. He was known for slipping in big races. In the 1,000 meters, his final Olympic race, he skated with no expectations—and set a world record. The gold medal became the punch line for his new story.

An old story can be so subtle. It is an insistent monologue that no one else but us hears, and, too often, it defines the small moments that are so critical.

Our fear story is all about the *but*.

"I would love to travel internationally, *but . . .*"

"I always thought that I would achieve partner, *but . . .*"

"I would have spent more time doing what I love, *but* . . ."

What if we traded all the *but*s for a new story of who, what, where, when, why, and how we most want to be?

Trading your old story for a better one is a fundamental act of fearlessness. It involves letting go of deep feelings in light of new facts, moment by moment.

In your story, you are a hero—a main character who believes in something bigger than yourself. If that bigger something is fear, it's time to get a new story.

Embracing your new story is like acting, the way Academy Award–winning actress Jodie Foster describes it: "You get to live out things that you're afraid of, and you get to say, 'Well, maybe I can get to the end of it and survive it intact, and I can be the hero of my own story.' It's kind of a way of exorcising fear."[5]

Our families often inspire our self-stories, and that's not always a good thing. Here's a time when I had to trade my old story for a new story to resolve my guilt about how we were raising our daughters.

My parents are close to us, and in their value system, being a good parent means being with your kids. Not long ago, when my daughters were on the cusp of adolescence, I took a business trip to Florida, Arizona, Pennsylvania, and New York. Normally, I don't go more than three days without seeing my family, so no touchdown in Atlanta was unique. I called my mom to check in en route to one of the cities.

I shared with her my excitement about the previous event and upcoming engagements, and I could hear Mom's ears perk up.

"Oh," she replied, "so you won't be home until Thursday?"

What I heard was, "Molly, are you sure you're with your girls enough?"

Since she is my greatest female role model, this question gave me serious pause. Guilt was the old story pulling me where

I didn't belong. I was not reliving my mother's life, and my girls weren't retracing my steps at the same age. My new story was just that: mine. We all have our own stories, old and new. My way of going through life is guided by my purpose: to connect, inspire, and lead with creative courage and optimism.

You can see how the old story/new story ties in with the previous trade (defensiveness to curiosity). I felt defensive when my mom questioned my work schedule. But in that moment, I also questioned what my feeling of guilt was telling me. And this led me to being more curious about my mom's concerns and talking about them more openly together, which led to greater closeness between us.

Your story unfolds moment by moment, and it can be framed by limiting beliefs. This is an open invitation for fear to move in rent free. There's little room for that to happen in your new story.

Along with speaking and writing, I often consult with highly competitive teams that are struggling to move forward. Often the roots of their dysfunction are deeply ingrained self-limiting beliefs.

I use a set of open-ended questions that I learned at the Johnson & Johnson Human Performance Institute (HPI) to help team members identify their old stories and begin to envision powerful new ones. Using the same questions will anchor you in the present and help you see yourself at a crossroads of old and new:

1. Set a target: I want to be more engaged with . . .

   _____

2. Set an intention: This is important to me because . . .

   _____

3. Understand your choice: If I continue on my present path, I expect . . .

_____

4. Introduce a new story: From now on, I will . . . [6]

_____

The power of revising your story is evident in novelist Karen Thompson Walker's TED Talk about reading fear.[7] Through the true story of a shipwreck, she demonstrates how we tell our stories through two main viewpoints: that of a scientist with cool judgment and facts and that of an artist willing to get caught up in vivid details and emotions. The best story weaves together facts and emotions to bring people to a new understanding of the world. That's the new story I'm talking about, and Walker suggests reading our fears to help absorb and transcend them and pursue our purpose.

"Read in the right way, our fears are an amazing gift of the imagination, a kind of everyday clairvoyance, a way of glimpsing what might be the future when there's still time to influence how that future will play out," she says. "Properly read, our fears can offer us something as precious as our favorite works of literature: a little wisdom, a bit of insight, and a version of that most elusive thing—the truth."

In telling your new story, you erase limiting beliefs and make room for greater fearlessness.

Trade Bad Stress for Good Stress

Don't you love it when you get a second wind? Scientists are fascinated with this phenomenon too. They are trying to dissect why and how, as we become increasingly tired and stressed, we cross a tipping point into an exhilarating energy that makes us feel even stronger than when we started. Scientists continue to study whether we may be capable of an infinite number of "winds" that we can access—if we just keep pushing.[8]

A second wind can be the product of trading bad stress for good stress. I experienced this through reinventing my career.

Bad stress happens when you are going through the motions following a purpose outside your beliefs. Good stress happens when you are pushing through to your personal mission.

I made a strategic change from the stress of sports representation (serving individual performers) to the stress of running my own business (serving thousands of people). I traded the stress of being absent at home and a consistent paycheck for the stress of spending more time at home and uncertain compensation.

Here's what made the difference for me and gave me my second wind: I was leaving bad stress that was draining me and claiming good stress that energized me.

Making this trade helped build my fearlessness. I had pushed past that tipping point and tapped major energy on the other side. The major outcome for me was greater personal balance.

But how do you pass from the familiar bad stress to the second wind?

One of the fundamental skills of fearlessness is intentionality. It means getting very clear and focused on what you need to be doing in the moment.

Intentionality helps you laser in on the small steps that fulfill your purpose. Sometimes those steps are not clear. It's easy to get caught up in someone else's agenda or get distracted.

Here's a simple way to visualize bad stress versus good stress related to your intentions. This works especially well if you are a person who says yes too quickly, if you take on tasks and projects because you want to be liked, or if you are addicted to doing too much.

Make a list of 10 things in your life that currently stress you out. These can be your work, various people, family obligations, or other things.

Reflect on your list. Mark the stressors you have control over—that is, those that you can do something about.

Now draw a big circle. Inside it, draw a small circle.

In the small circle, put the stressors that you have control over.

In the outer ring, put the rest of your list.

Your energy is represented by one of the circles, and it's up to you to pick a target.

Do you want to spread your energy wide to include all the stressors, regardless of whether you can make a difference? The outer ring is full of bad stress—the uncontrollables in life—and energy is wasted there.

Wouldn't it make more sense to focus your energy on the small circle at the center, the stressors you can influence? Those have the potential to be good stressors because they present challenges that you can possibly solve. Your attitude and effort can influence the outcome of those stressors. The center target is the portal to your second wind.

A circle also symbolizes how stress and fear follow each other without end. Stress will lead to fear, and fear will lead to stress if we keep focusing on the stress that we can't do anything about.

There will always be things that stress you that you can't push out of your life completely. The trade for good stress helps you focus on the work that leads to a second wind—and fear-lessness.

Philosopher and psychologist William James observed that people stay in bad stress because they don't know good stress. A second wind, he said, is a "source of strength habitually not taxed at all, because habitually we never push through the obstruction, never pass those early critical points."

When I read "habitually," I think "fearfully." It's taxing to rewire habits to greater fearlessness.

Try trading bad stress for good stress in small moments to build your source of strength. You will notice that as you take control of what you can change, you will have more courage to take on greater projects related to your purpose.

Keep going, and your second wind will help you make progress fearlessly.

Trade Words for Action

> *Do the thing you fear most,*
> *and the death of fear is certain.*
> —Mark Twain

> *It always seems impossible until it's **done**.*
> —Nelson Mandela

Do is so important. That's because "fearing less" is a verb, not a noun. It involves moving beyond thinking and talking. Without action, there is no demonstration of fearing less.

Think about how actions define our character and values. Let me give you a couple of personal examples.

My dad didn't have to tell me his main priority. He turned down a promotion, and I knew it was because the better job would have taken him away from us more. When he said no, he was showing us his priority was time with us: my mom, my twin brothers, and me.

Actions always express priorities, and my mom's actions showed me her priority was other people. My mom is one of the most selfless people I know. As a special needs teacher in the Lansing area public schools, my mom often encountered people who were dealing with tough circumstances. She knew every one of her students by name, and she was constantly filling boxes with the clothes my brothers and I had outgrown so that a needy student would have a jacket for the harsh Michigan winter. It was the same way she was always there for us. My mom was constantly on the go, but I can't remember her missing a single one of my tennis matches. Her actions showed me what mattered most to her.

Taking meaningful action is what I emphasize in my work, not just in this book. When audience members approach me after a speech to tell me how fired up they are, I remind them to choose one or two things that they can change and to formulate what steps they will take to get to their goal. To effect real change, your excitement needs to drive new behavior. You need to adopt a grab-and-go attitude, meaning that you have taken hold of the inspiration you need and you are moving with intention to new (or renewed) purpose. Words aren't enough. Actions are the proof of fearlessness.

The big outcomes result from taking charge of your life emotionally, physically, mentally, spiritually and relationally. It means stepping up to the hard process of taking necessary action. Fearless people transform their lives and the lives of others because they don't wait for things to happen to them and they don't give up when obstacles arise.

Our fundamental fearlessness is rooted in what we do. Talking about our purpose is nothing without meaningful action. How often do we see companies' big bold mission statements with core values like innovation, risk taking, and creativity, but we never see them put those values in action? Our words mean little when they do not align with our purpose and inspire our actions.

It's important to dig deeper. Before you trade words for action, it's critical that those words are the right ones. Purpose is everything, and a mission statement is a terrific way to stay focused on your why. If you decide to create a mission statement, which I recommend that you do, then the words in your mission statement have the potential to carry great weight.

Your mission statement captures why you are here. One way to back into this is to think about who you are when you are at your best, your truest self.[9] Thinking back to that time, ask yourself these questions:

"What matters most?"

"What makes life worth living?"

"What are my deepest values?"

"What makes me proud of myself?"

"What legacy do I want to leave behind?"

It's important to remember that there are no right answers. Personal mission statements take work and time. A personal mission statement can capture your essence when you are at peak performance. It is at these moments that you know what your best looks and feels like. Your personal mission statement reflects who you are and who you want to be, at your best. Here are more questions that helped me write my statement:

"How do I lead when I am my best self?"

"How do I think when I am my best self?"

"How do I react and recover when I am my best self?"

"Who am I emotionally, mentally, spiritually, physically, and relationally when I am my best self?"

"What is the best version of myself in my main roles [family member, friend, employee, leader, or some other role]?"

———

I LEARNED THIS approach from Dr. Jim Loehr, the chair and co-founder of the Johnson & Johnson Human Performance Institute (HPI), who has worked with some of the most elite athletes in the world and hundreds of executives in the highest echelons of business. It was completely transformative for me.

My mission statement resulted from devoting concentrated time planning and strategizing around my passions, talents, and experience. I worked hard to choose the right words. I wanted these words to be active and vivid. This is my mission statement: "To connect, inspire, and lead with creative courage and optimism."

I return to those 10 words as I plan my actions—my goals, decisions, schedules, spending, relationships, almost everything. My mission statement helps me determine which actions to take. As I go through my day, it is the filter I use to choose how I spend my time and resources.

When a new business opportunity arises, for example, I ask myself if I am connecting with creative courage and optimism. When a charitable request comes in, I decide how well it fits with inspiring and leading with creative courage and optimism. When I choose people to work with me, I think about how they can help me carry out my mission statement and how this work aligns with their purpose too.

The verbs *connect, inspire,* and *lead* are the actions I see myself doing. Connect, inspire, and lead are my *what*.

Creative courage and optimism make up the style and hallmark of my work. They are what set me apart. Creative courage and optimism are my *how*.

My work is in the present moment. I know the culmination of the small moments focused on my purpose will, over time, lead to a greater outcome. That's the power of optimism. Creative courage is one reason I am writing this book. This project stretches me to think differently and to share my experiences fearlessly with you so that you can foster fearlessness through the tools that resonate with you. I can't give you the words that will drive the actions that will help you practice fearlessness, but my optimism and creative courage can help you understand the importance of finding the right words that capture *your* purpose and seeing the small opportunities to trade those words for meaningful actions.

To sum up, fearlessness begins with understanding your purpose—your *why*. Your mission statement sums up your purpose with your *what* (meaningful actions) and *how* (the words that describe your unique style).

We get stuck when we confuse *how* for *what*. Thinking and talking about *what* makes us different and special is an important part of the process, but once we have a consensus on *how*, the only way we are going to move to results is by taking action.

How is never enough without *what*.

And *how* and *what* don't matter at all without *why*.

When we are grounded in purpose, fearlessness becomes a habit. Fearless people don't dwell on what's important because we're too busy doing it, and the sum of those small actions creates the great outcome of fulfilling our purpose.

Trade Comfort for Clarity

Fear and comfort often go hand-in-hand. I saw this over and over as a sports agent, when I met with the parents of those teenage athletes who had the potential to become professionals in their sports.

This is not a scenario that most parents prepare for. It's both wonderful and excruciating to see your child face a once-in-a-lifetime opportunity to sign a contract that could make him or her very wealthy. It's easy to fear making the wrong decision.

I saw parents whose desire for comfort made them trust agents who did not act in their best interest. I saw young athletes agreeing to deals without any concern for where they would be in 10 years. "Someday I will think about that" is the way they comforted themselves.

I always tried to give these parents and athletes my most sensible advice to help them make the best decision. They needed a perspective that wasn't comfortable as much as it was clear. Sometimes the best I could do was model the truth.

"Everyone wants a piece of your son, and it's so scary because you have no idea whom to trust," I would say. "You need someone who can take your child and this once-in-a-lifetime situation and maximize this window of time. You have worked hard to be in this position. You have raised this young man who has this special opportunity, and now you need some arms around you too, to help you."

"Whether you sign with me or someone else, you need to ask some tough questions. You need to find out who has fired the agents you interview, and why. What teams won't do deals with this agent. I believe you want to get to the root of their relationships and their reputations. Because they become an extension of your entire family. You want to get to the root of how much they care about you when you are about to make them a lot of money and how much they care about you when you are injured and struggling to sign deals."

I would speak in hopes that in my clarity about their crossroads, they would take these questions and ask them of me and others and that, in turn, they would have the clarity to make the best choice that would lead to the best outcome for their child. I had to be prepared to answer honestly when they asked me those tough questions.

Sometimes I would see tears in the eyes of parents as they navigated this complicated and important road map. I understood their need for comfort, but I really wanted them to see how achieving clarity would lead to a better decision for their children.

I wanted them to channel Dara Torres.

Torres was a 12-time Olympic medalist who in 2008 was the only swimmer to represent the United States in five Olympic Games.[10]

In 2007, at age 40, she won the 100-meter freestyle at the U.S. Nationals. On top of that, she beat her own American 50-meter freestyle record. All this just 15 months after giving birth to her first child—and 26 years after she initially set the record. Then she won silver medals in all three of her events at the 2008 Summer Olympics.

Torres could have stayed mighty comfortable in her retirement, but she courageously stepped up to the odds and defied them. If anyone had doubted her, she definitely proved she still had what it took to compete. That much was crystal clear.

Comfort can signal that you don't want to change, even when the change could make you happier. I was comfortable as a sports agent because I knew what my clients needed, and I knew I could deliver.

But the older my kids got, the more I noticed that my comfort level with my job was changing. I began to realize what this comfort had made me sacrifice in terms of my family life. To find more balance, I had to find clarity. So I risked my comfort level to ask my boss if I could leave the office at 3 p.m. and be accessible on my cell phone so I could be physically present with my girls. It was a 24/7 environment anyway, so it felt like an easy yes.

I also asked for a more structured compensation package for my team of agents. They were negotiating base and bonuses for their athletes, but they couldn't get it for themselves. It didn't feel right.

In that step away from comfort, fearlessness can grow. You don't achieve clarity unless you ask. And when you ask, you understand that the answer could be no.

And the answer I got was no. *No* is never comfortable, but it certainly brought me clarity. And it was a small moment that created a big outcome.

That *no* showed me what was not possible as far as my satisfaction with my job. *No* motivated me to get clear on my purpose, which, in turn, led me to start my own business.

Clarity led to a better balance for my family and even greater job satisfaction because I was reaching so many more people who could benefit from my experiences.

Clarity involves work. It means collecting and sifting through practical advice. When you gather facts, you can detour better around your fears.

Will you choose clarity over comfort as a way to achieve fearlessness?

ANCHORING YOUR VALUES

*It's not hard to make decisions when
you know what your values are.*
—Roy E. Disney, nephew of Walt Disney

A t the heart of fearless living is a sense of purpose. The values that inspire your purpose must be anchored within you to guide your reactions and decisions in the small moments. Every small moment revolves around the core understanding of your values and the work that you are meant to do. These chapters will help you make those moments count.

Values guide how you tell your story and protect your mission. Values alert you to opportunity. Values are the reason that success is not an accident.

Affecting lives in positive ways has always been an important value for me. As a sports agent, I focused on maximizing opportunities on and off the field for the individual athletes, coaches, and broadcasters I represented. It was deeply intense work that depended on an awareness of my clients' needs on a 24/7 basis. But when I saw these athletes and coaches at their speaking engagements in front of attentive audiences, I saw the exponential impact of connecting with and serving groups instead of individuals. My value of reaching and inspiring people beckoned me to a new arena and broader relationships.

Listening to my core values helped me take the first risky steps to the career I have today that satisfies my values in a fulfilling way.

Anchoring your values will knit meaningful actions to your deepest beliefs and help you seize small moments in which your authentic self learns to shine without fear. Values are the roots of fearlessness.

The following five trades will teach you new habits to identify and to practice your values. Build a priceless compass for confronting your greatest fears.

Trade Insecurity for Authenticity

> *"Authenticity is a collection of choices*
> *that we have to make every day.*
> *It's about the choice to show up and be real.*
> *The choice to be honest.*
> *The choice to let our true selves be seen."*
> —Brené Brown, author of
> *The Gifts of Imperfection*

Authenticity creates security and confidence. Only you know your authentic self—your strengths, challenges, aspirations, and, yes, your fears. Authenticity identifies your business just as a fingerprint identifies you.

No one can give you authenticity; only you can claim it. When you take this step, you cease measuring yourself according to others' values, and you work on developing yourself to become even better.

I've seen elite performers become insecure. Getting to the highest level on a world stage doesn't guarantee security and confidence. Sometimes it causes those very things to crumble under the pressure. Athletes operate in a comparably small window of opportunity. At a moment's notice, an injury or a decision by someone in power can destroy their comfortable life and dial back all future plans.

The outliers know differently. They know the power of fearing less.

Sean Lee traded insecurity for authenticity in January 2016 when he decided to bench himself as his team, the Dallas Cowboys, prepared for a playoff game. The decision, he knew, would cost him a $2 million bonus.

This payout was contingent on his playing 80 percent of the time the Cowboys were on defense. Lee was at 82 percent going into the game; not suiting up meant his percentage would dip below the trigger point. No one told him his injured hamstring would keep him from the lineup; he made that gutsy call.

"It was me who decided to not play," Lee said. "I didn't feel like I would be effective enough to help the football team. I'm not going to disrespect my coaches and be out there not playing the right way."[1]

You could say this was no big deal. After all, Lee's decision came during the second year of a six-year deal worth up to $42 million. What's $2 million to a guy like him?

Here's what I know: insecurity usually is not about the amount of money. It's about something else that is missing, like respect or opportunity or validation. Something bigger than the self. About a deep value.

Lee's action demonstrated his value of being on a team. It sounds old-fashioned when so much money is at stake, but a team is supposed to be a group of individuals who sacrifice their personal needs and fears for the collective goals. Lee valued that objective more than money, so it made perfect sense for him to sit himself down.

In these small moments, when we demonstrate what is important to us, we claim our authenticity. People notice, I think partly because selfishness and insecurity are so common. As journalist Ross Jones wrote, "Dallas Cowboys linebacker Sean Lee clearly plays football for more reasons than money."[2]

———

WHAT SETS YOU apart? Do your differences make you feel insecure and fearful? I know that feeling.

I couldn't hide as a woman trying to rise to the top in a male-dominated profession (sports representation) who segued into another one (keynote speaking and business ownership). I let go of insecurity by no longer seeing my gender as an obstacle. When I saw that being a woman was an asset, I claimed the authenticity that steered me through small moments of fearlessness to big outcomes.

And there were tons of small moments. Sports representation is all about service, and as a female sports agent, I could connect in ways that my male peers could not. Gift baskets to athletes' wives? Check. Advice to them about a feverish baby? Got it. Order red wine at a bar meeting instead of whiskey? That's how I roll.

My highest-performing clients were often authentic to the point of eccentricity. John Smoltz, for instance, told me how people called him a geek in high school because he obsessively practiced pitching against a strike zone taped to an exterior wall of his parents' house. He didn't understand behaviors that weren't purposeful, and he sure wasn't going to quit what was working for him. That authenticity ultimately led him to induction in the Baseball Hall of Fame.

The more small moments of authenticity that you rack up, the more your confidence will grow and the more opportunities you will see for greater fearlessness. For me, I noticed insecurity in the way I was comparing myself to impossible standards. I no longer worried about the gap between my sports experiences and what a Major League pitcher felt like taking the mound in Game 7. Not many among sports agents did.

I wasn't concerned about wearing a suit the way the guys did because that wasn't my style. I didn't have to dress the way they dressed to be a badass, nor did I actually need to be a badass. Over the course of many, many small moments, I came to understand that being my best self would cover that and more.

When you can be yourself and run with it, you're no longer carrying the burden of insecurity and fear. The breeze you feel is fearlessness.

Trade Status for Legacy

For 10 years, Carla Harris worked on some of Morgan Stanley's largest initial public offerings. During a transaction in the dot-com bubble of the early 2000s, she faced a quandary full of fear.

If she listened to her gut and gave her client the best advice, she might lose the client and quite possibly its large parent company. Or she could preserve the status quo and perhaps the market would take the blame for the failure.

What should she do? And was there an opportunity to trade status for legacy?

Here's how she tells the story:

> It was a deal that had lots of demand on the face of it, but the market didn't reflect that demand. Normally when there is demand, we get lots of feedback. That feedback gives us clarity in pricing the deal. No feedback gave us the impression that some investors were going to flip the stock. They were looking to make a quick buck and get out, and by doing that, the stock might open high and then drop like a stone. No one wants that to happen.
>
> I had met the client only briefly before all this. I knew my client's company was owned by a large important company. I knew my firm could go in and tell the client that we could not price this transaction. If we did that, they could leave us and go to a competitor, leaving me with a big problem with the parent company especially. I had fear about that.
>
> Or I could say what I felt. I could stick to my convictions and not price it. By advising the client not to go public, we could wait for the market to catch up. That was risky.
>
> When a situation like this happens, I pray. Prayer helps me find clarity. I also listen and look for any evidence of a clear no. The absence of no tells me that fear is likely holding me back. My next step is to ask, "What's the worst that can happen by going forward?" When I get clear on that answer, I can make a move with confidence.
>
> I knew that if my plan failed, I could recover. I would think about what steps I had taken or not, what I had listened to or ignored. I would embrace the process and move forward, knowing that I wouldn't be the first to fail nor the last.

> In this case, I decided to lean into the fear and advise the client not to price it. We went forward with the riskier solution.
>
> The client accepted my recommendation. Feedback started to come in, and this ended up being the right call. In two months, we built on that open communication with the client. We did a road show and decided on a price point. The stock was offered in the October aftermarket, and it did beautifully.
>
> I was glad to have met the risk of losing that deal, to realize the fear that was holding me back, and to have the courage to speak from my heart.[3]

That was one moment that eventually led to a big outcome: today Carla Harris is vice chair of Morgan Stanley Global Wealth Management and its senior client advisor. She is also a speaker, gospel singer, and author of two books: *Expect to Win* and *Strategize to Win*.

One of the easiest fears to succumb to is the fear of losing status. It can be your income, job position, social rank, or anything you perceive as an important measuring stick to others.

Threats to status are often immediate and urgent. It's hard to step back and see the big picture. And it's so important to create space to consider your legacy—what you want people to ultimately remember you for. Your legacy is built on all the small moments that you string together.

I saw this as a kid with my dad, who sacrificed career advancement as a pharmaceutical rep because his legacy as a dad hinged on his spending time with us. His fearless example of trading status for legacy influenced my career reinvention many years later. No one has an unlimited opportunity to make a difference in a lifetime, and I wanted to do more than make life better for elite performers. I wanted to reach the most people I could with a positive message, even if it meant risking failure. Dad's example helped give me the courage to change careers.

When you trade status for legacy, you anchor your values in the big picture of your life. Like Harris, you can make decisions that may be hard in the short term, in a way that makes you proud of what you stand for, even if those decisions risk failure. In fact, you should expect that taking a stance for legacy will have high stakes.

By trading status for legacy, you cement your values. You can make difficult decisions in the moments that create big outcomes, even for generations to come.

Trade Entitlement for Humility

Imagine swimming in the ocean for more than two days straight, trying to cover 110 miles in cold, shark-infested waters. Every stroke, kick, and breath is a small action in a huge undertaking.

Diana Nyad was 64 when she made her final try at her life's dream of swimming from Cuba to Florida. For open water swimmers, this crossing is like a moon shot. Not only does it take a great deal of training and preparation, it also takes a huge supporting cast.

After four failed tries, Nyad had valid reasons to think that this time she was owed success. If she made it—if she was the first person to swim this route to Key West—she could be called the greatest ocean swimmer of all time. After all that patience and work, she was entitled to the glory.

That's not what happened, because she traded entitlement for humility. When Nyad reached shore—severely dehydrated, sunburned, disoriented, and exhausted—she shared this:

> I have three messages. One is: we should never, ever give up. Two is: you're never too old to chase your dream. Three is: it looks like a solitary sport, but it is a team.

"Wow," I thought in amazement as I watched the news coverage. She had endured nearly 53 solitary hours in the water, relying on mental tricks, such as counting her strokes in different languages and scrolling through her mental playlist of 85 songs. To an outsider like me, it appeared to be all about Nyad's incredible individual talent.

Yet she only used "I" once in her big message. "We," "you," and "team" were front and center. By trading entitlement for humility, she created room for an outcome that was much greater than her singular effort. By including others in her moment, Nyad anchored how much she valued inspiring others. She invited others to see themselves chasing their big dreams, and she celebrated the otherwise unsung heroes who supported her feat. She recounts those lessons and more in her appropriately titled autobiography, *Find a Way*.

Humility gets a bad rap. It's not the same as being meek or weak. It's certainly not fearful. Humility is a core value worth anchoring deep within you because it is a pathway to fearlessness.

When we are humble, we acknowledge authentically what we can and cannot do. We're not trying to puff ourselves up. We're not overpromising. There's no arrogance or selfishness. Humility is the state of knowing that it's not all about you. In fact, it's all about other people.

When you move through life's moments with humility instead of entitlement, you don't fear your truth. You claim it by fearing less. You begin to think that your own approval is more important than others'.

Sharing the credit can be scary. What if outsiders miss your importance? That is the fear that keeps people focused on themselves. When you stop hanging on so tight to what other people think, you can be fearless about standing up for what is important to you.

Atlanta Braves pitcher John Smoltz did this in his Baseball Hall of Fame induction speech:

> I remember sitting in the locker room at Tiger Stadium, a fish out of water, scared to death. . . . Alan Trammell came up to me and said, "Hi, I am Alan Trammell. Anything I can do for you, don't hesitate to ask. This house is your house." It was as if he had introduced and gave me a baton and said, "Now pay this forward every chance you can because this game has a chance to impact a lot of people."[4]

Trammell didn't have to calm a rookie's nerves. He was a star in his own right. Yet that small moment of encouragement to Smoltz paid huge dividends because Smoltz went on to play 21 seasons in the majors, building a stellar reputation as a pay-it-forward kind of guy, especially in his community work.

Nyad didn't have to share the spotlight with her 35-person support team of doctors, navigators, special equipment staff, divers, kayakers, and even a jellyfish expert who made sure she wouldn't get stung. By giving them credit, she was even more of a symbol of cooperation and human connection between two estranged countries. One big outcome was the United States invitation to join his diplomatic entourage in 2016 as relations with Cuba warmed.[5] She was picked for that team because her humble response to triumph cemented her commitment to teamwork. When you're trying to turn an enemy into an ally, Nyad is the perfect type of teammate.

Trading entitlement for humility produces a fearlessness that is contagious. Nyad's moment of glory included her team, and it sealed them as her allies and loyalists.

Look for small moments to practice this trade. We all need people who will help get us through the choppy waters of trying to live a life of greatest meaning and purpose.

Trade Adult Limits for Childhood Play

Fearlessness is already within most of us, in the bold playfulness we had as children—before we accepted the limits of adulthood.

An advertising campaign during the 2016 Olympics tapped into this feeling. Star sprinter Usain Bolt, basketball player Paul George, beach volleyball player April Ross, and tennis champion Serena Williams each had a shadow self—a kid who represented who they were when they were young.[6]

The mini-mes used their infectious joy for pure sport to push the celebrity athletes through tough workouts. "The best never lose that love" was the ad's slogan, and it was hard for anyone who grew up playing not to feel the ripple of childhood joy. No wonder Peyton Manning, for one, returned to his childhood football routine at his career peak. By drilling just the way he did in his days as a peewee player, he tapped into a simpler time.[7]

Think back on what that was like for you. Kids often have a natural fearlessness that is lost in adulthood. We learn to worry that we might fail or look dumb. Did that happen as a result of the small moments in your journey? Did your pure joy drip away as you grew up?

I reflect on the spoken word poetry of Azure Antoinette, with whom I had the pleasure of sharing a stage at a recent women's leadership event. Called "the Maya Angelou of the millennial generation," Antoinette was the closing speaker for the 2013 TEDWomen Conference. Her poem "Inner Voice" left an indelible mark:

> What did I do with my confidence?
> Where did I misplace the wilds in me that told me that any-
>   thing I wanted to accomplish could be done before my
>   mid-day nap?
> I have been looking in all the wrong places.
> I have been searching for my identity in pencil skirts that
>   would look just right, if my waist were a little tighter.
> I have been searching for the fearlessness of my youth in
>   cosmetics that sit just right on cheekbones that have
>   been engineered by Photoshop

Antoinette's voice captures perfectly the loss of her childhood fearlessness that she is trying to reclaim as an adult. What we experience as children can help shape what success and purpose look like to us today. When I speak to a group, one measure of success is seeing listeners laugh, cry, or both. These are such resonant reactions because when we were kids, laughter and tears were close to the surface. I want to connect with my audience in a profound way, and when I see them laugh or cry, I know I've done that.

Our childhood play is so important because it can point to our greatest passions and talents. If you are stuck without much purpose in your life, try looking back at what you enjoyed as a kid:

- "What did I do when there wasn't anything to do?"

- "Was there an activity that was so engrossing that I lost track of time and place?"

- "Did anyone ever say that I had a specific gift or talent?"

So much of my work is driven by my answers to those questions. Tree climbing has become a powerful metaphor and memory that drives my fearlessness.

Not everybody climbs trees the way I could. The taller the tree, the better it felt to succeed. Some trunks were hard to grip, and getting a good hold was the only way to start.

I knew I might fall, and when I did, the other kids laughed. I shook it off. Failing made me double down and come up with more energy. I knew how to keep going, and I still do.

I climbed without any thought of how someone else would do it or if they would do it better. That was my joy: I knew I was enough. When you are enough, even when your inner voice might be tempted to tell you otherwise, you are fearless.

Those scraped knees from tree climbing signaled pain, but the blood and scars weren't worth worrying about. They were just proof that I was getting stronger by going higher. From playing, we learn discipline, and we gain the ability to recover.

When I got a little older, climbing trees gave way to more intellectual interests. I spent countless hours in bookstores reading about peak performance, studying the habits of people who pushed themselves to reach their potential, who had the guts to ask themselves hard questions.

This pursuit sparked new discoveries and courage. If inspiring peak performance and strategic influence is what I truly love, how can I make a living at it? How can I make my adult work mirror my childhood play?

Questions about childhood play can tap into your natural fearlessness, and answering them can recover your innate fearlessness.

When I am stuck in the daily grind, a few small directed moments of trading adult limits for childhood play will produce big results.

I reflect on trees as symbols of hopes and dreams. As a speaker and author, I try to model the power of belief so others see past the forest of expectations to the trees that each of us is called to climb. These specific challenges are unique to each of us, calling us to be confident that deep inside us, we have what we need for that climb.

You have it, I have it, we have it.

So what if people don't even see or recognize the tree you are called to climb, or if they laugh when you tumble, or if they try to complicate your simple purpose. Protect your playfulness. Be fearless. Keep going.

Look down for your roots and up to the highest branches, and understand that your greatest strength is not bound by adult limits. Your childhood play, and its accumulated small moments of trial and error, anchored your fearlessness deep within you. It's still there.

Trade Certainty for Joy

By understanding and accepting that none of us can ever be entirely certain about events that will rock our world, we can move into a truer understanding of fearing less and creating more joy. When we convince ourselves that we need to be sure, that we need to minimize what we can't control, we decrease the room in our lives for our deepest happiness. The pursuit of certainty can prevent us from moving into our true purpose, where joy lives and fearlessness grows.

When you value certainty, you need fearlessness to push you out of your comfort zone. Big opportunities often require people to leave what they have always known for the *possibility* of joy.

In the business world, inventors are great examples of this trade. Joy Mangano, the inventor of the Miracle Mop, dedicated herself to pursuing her idea even though she was a divorced mom of three kids, with little capital. It was safer not to try to enter the market for household products. But she believed in her idea of a self-wringing mop so much that she took the risk.

Today Mangano has sold $3 billion in mops and other inventions on home shopping channels, breaking out as a TV personality on the strength of her passion for her mop and other inventions such as nonslip Huggable Hangers [8] The story of her success turned into the movie *Joy*.

In the movie, Mangano has a nightmare in which she is visited by her younger self, who says, "When you're hiding, you're safe because people can't see you. But funny thing about hiding: you're even hidden from yourself." Mangano takes this as a sign to fight for her ideas.

Joy is both her name and the result of her fearless passion for practical solutions to household pain points. She truly understands her market of money-conscious people, and she has a knack for seeing where products like hers fit in. People buy her inventions to improve their lives and because they sense her joy in inventing something that she believes will truly help them. Her more than a hundred patents and trademarks have resulted from her willingness to move away from certainty and into a risky environment.

"You have to make a decision: Am I gonna be the person who takes the risk? Am I gonna be the person who says, 'I'm gonna start this business, and I'm gonna follow through with it no matter what the obstacles?'" she has said. "I kind of equate it to a woman having a baby. You go into the hospital, and you're having a baby. You can't say halfway through, 'I'm not gonna do this anymore!' You have to have the courage to finish. I view everything in life that way."

Her success demonstrates that people who take a leap of faith achieve a level of joy that they could not have experienced if they had stayed in their safe place of certainty.

The feeling of joy is aligned with clarity: when you are where you need to be, and you are going where you need to go, getting there is the most fulfilling part of the journey.

3

MAXIMIZING
YOUR FOCUS

When pulled in every direction,
you stay in the same spot.
—Anonymous

The best golfers plan their tournament schedules to peak for the four major championships. They strategize the best schedule of tournaments around the courses that best fit their games.

Winning a title is the result of many small moments of maximizing their focus. These moments are what losing hinges on too. Jordan Spieth blew the 2016 Masters by failing to take a single extra deep breath before an important putt.[1]

Distractions are everywhere, and time is limited. A big part of fearlessness is maximizing your focus on the small moments in which your attention is diverted and your energy is sapped.

When we maximize our focus, we reframe our decisions around the understanding that we have unique gifts that we are in charge of exercising, and doing this work naturally means saying no to, or negotiating, tasks and duties that others would like us to take on.

Maximizing my focus has meant that I accept fewer invitations to speak that are not in my sweet spot. If I am asked to do a keynote on a topic I do not feel that I own, I pass. My focus is maximized around my mission: to connect, inspire, and lead with creative courage and optimism.

Facebook founder Mark Zuckerberg said this about fearlessness in innovation: "We go mission-first, then focus on the pieces we need and go deep on them and be committed to them." That's a great description of the maximum focus that these next five trades will help you create, one moment at a time.

Trade Excuses for Accountability

Guts and fearlessness produce a vivid picture of possibility. That's what attracted people to Jim Valvano.

Jimmy Valvano ("Jimmy V") first made headlines as the coach of North Carolina (NC) State's scrappy basketball team that won the 1983 national championship. Jimmy V was a big-mouthed, bigger-than-life character whose enthusiasm radiated like the sun. But his lasting legacy is the way he dealt with terminal cancer.

Jimmy V had a job to do, and he did it. He took what made him a good coach—the ability to inspire his players to never give up—and held himself to the same standard.

He didn't want to die. He feared dying. He made the choice to live out his best example every remaining minute. He had a conversation with cancer that went something like this: "I know what you are, and I know who I am, and I'm going to do exactly what I need to, regardless of what you're up to."

For Jimmy V, accountability began with structure and commitment, and a keen perspective on the present moment.

There were three daily acts for which he held himself accountable. "Number one is laugh. You should laugh every day. Number two is think. You should spend some time in thought. Number three is you should have your emotions moved to tears, could be happiness or joy. But think about it. If you laugh, you think, and you cry, that's a full day. That's a heck of a day."[2]

He maintained other simple levels of accountability. "I always have to think about what's important in life to me, and they are these three things: where you started, where you are, and where you're going to be. Those are the three things that I try to do every day."

The product of those small moments of accountability was huge. "You do that seven days a week, you're going to have something special," he said of his three-a-day strategy.

Jimmy V's life ended at age 47, but because he refused to make excuses, his legacy was so much more than his diagnosis. He used his platform and celebrity to raise awareness for cancer research, and his foundation has attracted more than $150 million to help find a cure.[3] His no-excuses attitude has influenced countless followers. "Coach V lives on in me," said one of his star players, Thurl Bailey. "It's amazing how his legacy has continued to carry on. What he stood for is a 'never quit, never give up' attitude. That's what I live by. That's what my kids live by."

Fearless people like Jim Valvano are very much in the present moment. When you are fearless, you understand that you are the boss of you right now. You can choose excuses, or you can stay accountable.

Entrepreneurs are a great example of trading excuses for accountability. A recent survey showed that about a third of current entrepreneurs got their start while working full-time for someone else.[4] They couldn't make progress if they used their day job as an excuse. Instead, they became accountable to double duty, reminding themselves that the short-term sacrifice of time and energy was positioning them for entrepreneurial success. Working full-time and starting up a business allows entrepreneurs to cash a steady paycheck, build a potential client base, network, develop better business skills, and acquire more knowledge about their field and self-employment prospects.

In any work culture, excuses can run rampant. You know the team members who always have reasons and explanations for breaking promises and missing deadlines. When we make excuses, we allow external factors to control our actions. In that space, fear can take hold because we fear what we do not control. By choosing accountability, we commit to striving for our best and making optimal decisions in every small moment. By owning our actions (including our mistakes), we increase our sense of self, our sphere of influence, and our understanding of our potential. That greater awareness feeds into fearlessness.

You probably will find that telling your new story and becoming more authentic requires you to give up excuses. Excuses can't coexist with your new story driven by your mission statement.

Accountability can lead, as it did for Jimmy V, to fearlessly claiming your authentic identity, recognizing your best tools and tactics, and staking out your mission.

"Cancer can take away all my physical abilities," he said. "It cannot touch my mind, it cannot touch my heart, and it cannot touch my soul. And those three things are going to carry on forever."

Trade Regret for Responsibility

When I look back, will I regret not facing this fear? Meredith Leapley makes a lot of decisions by asking herself that. It's

helped her push through fear and become a very successful business owner

Leapley was only 26 when she came to Atlanta with no college degree and few professional connections. Fear didn't stop
her. She established a commercial interior general contracting
firm, and within 15 years, Leapley Construction (generated
more than $66 million in revenue with top corporate clients
such as the Coca-Cola Company, Norfolk Southern, Georgia
Power, and Turner Properties.[5]

When we spoke about fearlessness, Leapley described an
approach that I call "trading regrets for responsibility." During
her remarkable rise to business success, Leapley noticed that today's fears lead to tomorrow's regrets.

That pattern has influenced her decisions about work and
other important parts of her life. When faced with an important decision, Leapley imagines any regrets that she might have
in the future.

These imagined regrets have driven her to take responsibility for doing the next right thing. Here's one example of how
that helped her.

"When Coca-Cola called me and asked if I could do a big
project, the chatter in my head was, 'I don't really have the experience,'" she recalled.[6] "I was scared, and I didn't know if this
would work out."

She asked herself if she would look back on this opportunity one day and regret turning Coca-Cola down. Or regret saying yes. "Answering that question made me uncomfortable to
the point that I could find a path to fearlessness," she said.

She decided to use her discomfort as motivation. She said
yes to Coke. "Ultimately, that project led to other big companies' wanting to work with us," she said. "When you see an
open door and step through it, it might not be exactly the right

decision, but if it's not, it will lead to something else that is. When you listen to your gut, you're going to learn something."

Leaning into her fear and examining potential regrets gave Leapley more clarity about what was important to her. Her decisions solidified her values of integrity, persistence, and hard work. These moments created the big outcome of making her firm one of the fastest-growing woman-owned companies in Atlanta, Georgia.

Leapley shared a personal moment that changed her life and related to trading regret for responsibility. In early adulthood, before she had found her niche in business, she stepped on a scale holding a pumpernickel bagel spread with cream cheese. The weight that registered upset Leapley so much that she tossed the bagel. "I am done," she told herself. "I will do whatever it takes to get this weight off."

In that moment, Leapley understood how much she would regret the small moment of consuming that many calories. She feared not being able to gain control over that part of her life and health.

A health coach helped her develop new behavior patterns and the discipline and confidence to keep herself healthy. She saw how internal changes—the way she thought about herself—drove external changes, such as working to achieve better health. The reverse was also true: fearless actions could create greater feelings of fearlessness. She took the chance and moved from her home area of Washington, D.C., to a new city to establish a new perception of herself.

Leapley's experiences are so valuable because they speak to the power of regret in our lives. Looking back on my career as a sports agent, I regret I did not push my clients to consider the future and work their way back from perceived regrets, as Leapley does.

I trade those regrets for the responsibility of being the agent of my own purpose and helping others achieve their best selves now. I have learned to ask myself, and I teach others how to ask themselves, the harder questions related to values and what comes next:

- "If my career ended tomorrow, what do I see as my legacy?"

- "What are the top three things I want to accomplish after I do all that I can where I am now?"

- "Does what I am doing now reflect what I most want to be known for when I look back on my choices?"

This is also true: Regret grows from the conversations that you did not have. Regret says, "I wish . . ."

Responsibility moves that conversation into the present and future. It says, "I was . . . I am . . . I will . . ."

Like my friend Meredith Leapley, let your regrets lead to taking responsibility for your next small moment. Keep practicing the small acts of owning your nows. When you trade regret for responsibility, you use the lessons of the past and dreams of the future to fulfill your purpose in the present. That is the stuff fearlessness is made of.

Trade Passivity for Strategy

Only those who dare to fail greatly can ever achieve greatly.
—Robert F. Kennedy

In the fall of 2008, the fast-food chain Popeyes was about to roll out a new branding campaign when the stock market crashed.

CEO Cheryl Bachelder realized she was in the worst economy she had ever seen, and no one would criticize her leadership team if they held off on the rollout—indeed, shareholders might praise her for wise stewardship. But before Popeyes did the expected, Bachelder wanted to make sure she was acting strategically.

Franchisees always have been the heart of Popeyes's success, and in an economic downturn, these 300+ stakeholders had the most to lose. Their relationship with leadership was strained to say the least. Bachelder was the fifth CEO in seven years, and the latest franchisee satisfaction score was 76 percent. "Don't expect us to trust you anytime soon," one franchisee had told her.

Her leadership team had created the branding campaign as a way to rebuild trust and achieve a key goal of building a distinctive brand. Now would the leadership team have the courage to move forward and roll out? "We can't serve our people well if we are not performing well" was part of Bachelder's message. "Our success, and that of our shareholders, has to be based on the franchisees' success."

Her leadership team traded passivity for strategy. The brand campaign proceeded amid risk—and it worked. Satisfaction among franchisees in 2013 was measured at 95 percent.[7] Her leadership had led to market share gains of 6 points, improved guest ratings, and increased restaurant margins (400 basis points in five years). In six years, Popeyes's enterprise market cap—the measure of its total value—had grown from $300 million to over $1 billion, and by the end of 2013, its systemwide revenues were $2.4 billion.[8]

When we wait for something to happen, fear can grow like weeds. That's passivity. Strategy is planning for what you want and going to get it.

Dare to Serve is Bachelder's leadership philosophy and the title of her book that tells the story behind the revival of the Popeyes brand. Trading passivity for strategy is particularly important as the competition increases and the stakes (like the ones Bachelder faced in the recession) rise. For sports agents, passivity is kryptonite. Because the number of sports agents exceeds the pro athletes who need representation, no athlete ever came to us. We had to pursue them. We had to make the connection and work to keep it.

Passivity often comes from fear of failure, a feeling that you don't belong at the table, that you have no business rolling the dice until someone hands you a pair and tells you it's OK. Fearlessness doesn't work that way. It requires strategy and trust in that strategy.

Fearlessness requires action, and it is acquired by taking action. Fearless people recognize the boundary and cross it by trying. Soccer star Mia Hamm tells her three daughters that to win, they must first participate. They must take that first step. And to do that, they must believe they are worth it. Action and belief go hand-in-hand. "When you make that decision, you are worth it," Hamm says.[9]

Bachelder told me that fear of what other people think seems to afflict women leaders particularly. They get trapped by living up to other people's purpose, not their own, and they stay trapped by their small moments and decisions that reinforce the status quo. Bachelder broke from passivity by embracing strategy: the opinions of others became less important once she identified and committed to live out her own purpose.

"In moments of fear, I look at my experiences and beliefs," Bachelder has said. "I have years of experience growing brands and confidence that my approach at Popeyes will work. I believe that a company that invests during down times can still succeed and that taking that risk when others do not can lead to even greater success. My experience supported the decision."

Passivity rooted in the fear of failure can be reframed. Just look anywhere in Silicon Valley and you'll find the "fail fast and often" mentality. Companies such as Google award bonuses to employees who think big and have the courage to kill their great idea if it isn't working. Google understands that transformative innovation results from a culture of risk taking and its pile of failed ideas, so the company rewards the thinkers who help cull the bulletproof projects from those with problems.

"A lot of people still think of failure as a sign of personal incompetence and try to avoid it at all cost," said Andrew Filev, CEO and founder of Wrike, a project management software firm.[10] "But when you view building a business as a series of experiments, you start to see failure as an inevitable step in the process."

Beware of complaining and whining, which are common signs of passivity. Don't wait for things to come to you.

Be in the present with your strategy, and seize the small moments to take action that will drive your purpose. That's how you build up the muscle called "fearlessness."

Trade Impulse for Self-Discipline

I have two kinds of problems: the urgent and
the important. The urgent are not important,
and the important are never urgent.
—Dwight D. Eisenhower

In the summer, my family would travel to our cabin on Little Long Lake in northern Michigan. Calling it a "lake" was a stretch. "Pond" was more like it. We would drive up there, and we always looked forward to stopping at an ice cream shop along the way. The promise of delicious cones made the hours in the car a whole lot more bearable.

"Who wants ice cream?" Dad would yell to us in the back.

"I do, I do, I do," my brothers and I would reply.

"What kind?"

" Cookiesandcreambluemoonchocolatechip!"

"Awesome!" Dad would say as we approached the exit . . .

. . . and watched it fly by.

"Dad?"

"I was just wondering what kind of ice cream you like," he would say.

This may sound mean, but Dad taught us the value of trading impulse for discipline. Sometimes he turned on the air-conditioner when it got hot. Sometimes he refused to take the simple step of turning that knob.

"You need to be uncomfortable," he would say on the days we didn't stop, on the days the temperature stayed high.

As our images of tasty ice cream dripped away, as sweat crept down our skin and dampened our T-shirts, we learned to embrace self-discipline. It helped that we had parents whose experience we respected and trusted. It also wasn't as hard as it sounds because we already had experienced the benefits of his toughening.

———

FOR MY BROTHERS, it was flying lessons that instilled self-discipline. They learned the importance of details and patience— crossing every "t" and dotting every "i" as they prepared. Their discipline helped them master the fundamentals, and it paved the way to earning pilot licenses as teenagers and careers later as pilots in the military and commercial airlines. I poured my heart into tennis, relying on the discipline my parents had helped instill in me to get me through long practices and tough matches. Tennis taught me to stick with the process and stay mentally and physically disciplined even when the pressure was high.

We enjoyed celebrating and sharing each other's successes, which we saw as the direct result of hard work and trading impulse for self-discipline. Through this habit, we gave ourselves room to push through to achieve what we most wanted. We were equipped to achieve larger things, even if they were harder, and not settle for what was quick and easy.

As time went by, I leveraged this toughness. I leaned into moments of discomfort in my tennis matches, in college classes, in tough jobs, and with demanding bosses. These little moments of being uncomfortable, of resisting impulse, helped me achieve the self-discipline necessary to keep working for bigger outcomes.

Ice cream beckons to us all day long. Instant gratification is in the palm of our hands. Marketers play to our fear of missing out (FOMO) with messages like "only one more in stock" and "limited time only" and "your discount extended 24 hours."

Brain chemistry is at work when we are deciding between impulse and discipline. This is why your purpose is so important.

Our brains release dopamine when we achieve goals, and it improves attention, memory, and motivation. This is true no matter what the size of the goal. We love checking items off a to-do list. This "completion bias" helps us keep moving forward, and it also invites impulsiveness.[11] You might have experienced this after a busy day in which you did not get anything of significance done. The easy short-term tasks became an impulse distracting you from the more important long-term goal.

Don't get stuck in the dopamine drip of check-off items that have little long-term significance. A great way to trade impulse for discipline is to spend a few key moments reviewing your tasks against your mission statement and commit to your top priorities. You don't have to fear missing out when you are focused on what is most important.

Fearlessness involves rejecting the idea of instant gratification. Fearlessness requires, and results from, discipline. When we get easily what we think we want, we expect that what we really want will come to us the same way. But it will not be instant or easy.

You can't hit snooze and truly live your purpose. When you wake up and get out of bed, you trade momentary discomfort for more time to pursue your purpose. Fearlessness is connected to discomfort. The discomfort of small moments will create a big outcome because you will be more disciplined and you will not fear missing out.

On those hot summer days when I allow myself an ice cream cone, I taste what my dad taught us so well: impulse does not rule a fearless person.

Trade Generalities for Specifics

"Don't become a wandering generality. Be a meaningful specific." This quote from Zig Ziglar gently helped steer me from a big broad dream for my life to the daily specifics to which I really needed to pay attention. Mr. Ziglar taught me the power of trading generalities for specifics, to think of my purpose taking shape as I lived the small moments of life.

Raised in a family of 12 by a single mother, Ziglar suffered through the death of his father during the Depression. He eventually landed a job selling cookware, and after a supervisor helped him see that he could be a great salesman, Ziglar became one. His attitude made all the difference.

"I'm so optimistic I'd go after Moby-Dick in a rowboat and take the tartar sauce with me," he said more than once.

Ziglar left sales to go into motivational speaking, and in 1975, he published the bestseller *See You at the Top*, which has sold more than 1.7 million copies and is still in print.[12] He was THE name in motivational speaking when I was growing up and looking for any edge I could get in tennis, school, and life.

When I heard Mr. Ziglar was coming to Atlanta, I wrangled my way in to see him for a brief appointment. At the time, I was in one of my very first jobs out of college, selling sports instructional videos. I told someone in my emerging network that I had always wanted to meet Zig Ziglar. Not just any great motivational speaker. Specifically, Zig Ziglar. What happened next proved to me, at that early stage in my career, the power of voicing a goal—a specific goal.

One of my colleagues made the connection, and meeting Zig Ziglar became a reality. I was 22, and, as I explained to Mr. Ziglar, I wanted to be a speaker. That was my broad idea. While I felt like I always had something to say, my experience boiled down to having applied to speak at my high school commencement, working very hard on a speech, and then being turned down.

I can't imagine how much compassion Mr. Ziglar summoned not to laugh me out of the room. Instead of being condescending, he kindly told me the truth: I had no experience or authority to tell anyone much of anything.

Yet.

Ziglar was all about the now and the future. He was, after all, the person who said:

> You may not be where you want to be, but that's got nothing to do with your future. Your attitude, not your aptitude, will determine your altitude.

I hung on every word. This guru had dissected success to determine its most vital steps. Mr. Ziglar told me I needed to map out how I was going to get moving toward my goal. With his valuable feedback, I homed in on my two passions: speaking and the business of sports. I didn't have experience speaking (and realistically I couldn't say that a lot of people wanted to hear what I had to say at that point in my life!). I could, however, explore my passion for working in the field of sports. I didn't know if I would ever go into speaking, but I knew that working in sports was the other career path that piqued my interest and tapped into my passion. Even if I never got into speaking, I was relatively sure I could find contentment and purpose with this plan because of my love for athletic competition and appreciation for those who make it to the highest level.

After my 15-minute meeting with Mr. Ziglar, I plunged in. I wrote down concrete actions that would develop my rabid passion for sports. The general idea of what I thought I wanted to do was no longer on my mind. Instead, I concentrated on related specific actions in the here and now, and these actions focused on building my career in sports.

As I moved forward and kept going, I learned the truth of another Zig Ziglar quote:

> When you do the right things in the right way, you have nothing to lose because you have nothing to fear.

I have lived through the high-pressure negotiations and deals that high-performing salespeople like Zig Ziglar was so familiar with. These experiences revealed that fear isn't necessarily keeping us from making progress. Instead, fear occupies the gap left when we haven't made specific plans to become the person we want to be.

The way forward isn't made by big bounds. It's achieved incrementally, in small moments.

I wish Mr. Ziglar could read this and know how much his brief visit meant to me. It was a big outcome from what he surely considered a small moment. Zig Ziglar died in 2012. The investment he made in motivating others will always be his legacy. When he encouraged me to trade my generalities for specifics, he modeled the thinking that this book is based on:

> You never know when a moment and a few sincere words can have an impact on a life forever.

STRETCHING CRITICAL MOMENTS

Life shrinks or expands in proportion to one's courage.
—Anaïs Nin

So far you've read a lot about identifying moments in which we practice new habits that lead to remarkable results. But what if the moment itself can be expanded?

Extreme athletes and other peak performers do this all the time. They have learned to stretch critical moments, to see options and grab them in the heat of a conflict or crisis. Instead of pushing away fear during critical turning points, they embrace it.

Sometimes this skill is the difference between life and death. Mountain climber Sir Edmund Hillary, the first Western person to summit Mount Everest, noted this when he said, "The feeling of fear, as long as you can take advantage of it and not be rendered useless by it, can make you extend yourself beyond what you would regard as your capacity. If you're afraid, the blood seems to flow freely through the veins, and you really do feel a sense of stimulation."

It may not be Everest, but we're all climbing something. For most of us, stretching critical moments will help us think better on our feet. To say the right thing at the right time. To stand up for principle and speak up for what we need.

When your concentration is so intense that there is no room for fear, you find more of what you most need to meet the challenge at hand. Some people call this experience "flow," or you may have thought of it as "being in a zone."

You can't make a minute longer than 60 seconds, but you can make those increments of time bend.

Trade Scarcity for Opportunity

A breakthrough doesn't have to be a four-minute mile. It can be starting your own business. It can be asking for and getting a promotion. It can be starting an exercise regimen. Your breakthrough is what you have not done before, and it's an opportunity that you are striving for.

Breakthroughs are called that because we recognize a limit that has been set and accepted, creating a psychological barrier to going further. You're going to have to push through your fear to get there.

A lot of that fear is about not having enough of what you need to get to your opportunity. In the small moments of pursuing your breakthrough, there is so much room for fear. It can be paralyzing.

But accepting scarcity and mindfully trading it for opportunity produces absolutely remarkable results. It is a key trade that stretches critical moments. Here's a great example of what I mean.

How did illusionist and "endurance artist" David Blaine hold his breath underwater for more than 17 minutes?

In Blaine's case, the scarcity was oxygen. The opportunity was to connect with a national TV audience. Their attention was glued to the water tank on Oprah Winfrey's TV show; once Blaine submerged, the moments stretched out like hours. Success was possible only through fearlessness.

Underwater, Blaine leaned on his mental resources to stay still and slow his heart rate. He had undergone an intense physical conditioning regimen leading up to the attempt, but controlling his body depended on powerful mindfulness and relaxation techniques. Facing oxygen deprivation, he pushed his physical limits by stretching his thinking, moment by moment.

"I had to remain perfectly still and just relax and think that I wasn't in my body, and just control that," Blaine said later. His mantra was to "just hold and relax through all the pain."[1]

Like you probably, I have no intention to see how long I can hold my breath underwater. But I do have plans and dreams, hopes and desires to push past what I have accomplished.

———

SCARCITY CONFRONTED ME every day I worked as a sports agent. There were far more agents than there were coaches and athletes who needed representation. Coaches were under pressure to win in a very short period. They needed an agent to maximize their security—financial and otherwise—so they could focus on making the most of the opportunity to lead. Colleges staked their athletic reputations on their high-profile coaches, whose success depended on the chemistry and confidence of athletes not even old enough to rent a car.

Professional athletes had an even smaller window. They typically faced a very short period in which they could leverage their skills and peak performance for the maximum return. For every Hall of Fame veteran like John Smoltz, there were dozens of flameouts.

Scarcity was a natural driver in that environment, and it created a culture in which people did not share information and felt threatened by competition—a culture of fear.

As I learned to thrive in scarcity, I recognized that something big was missing. Sometimes I would see an athlete leave money on the table because he was loyal to his manager or wanted to stay in his community. I began to realize that these performers had moved beyond scarcity thinking to abundance and opportunity. Their sense of purpose expanded what was possible. Scarcity turned into opportunity because they consciously made it so.

When I chose to move from that ultracompetitive arena to become a speaker, author, and business owner, I learned that scarcity remains a driver in this world too. Every time I speak, I learn more about the power of stretching the critical moments that I have to connect with my audience. Time is precious, and when a company gives me an hour of its employees' time, that is a huge opportunity to share an important message.

I want to inject every morsel of time with my best effort and spirit, to motivate and inspire listeners to tackle purposeful behavioral changes. My best speaking comes from embodying what can be, not what isn't. When I can do that, my critical moments on stage stretch. I'm in the flow of my talk.

The biggest takeaway for me from Blaine's story is about the magical experience of achieving these big breakthroughs—to inhabit opportunity, not be shackled by scarcity.

It's not luck. It's about a lot of small moments in which we practice our concentration. These small moments of expanding time prepare us for surpassing our limits.

"It's practice, it's training and experimenting, while pushing through the pain to be the best that I can be," Blaine has said. "And that's what magic is to me."

Trade Urgency for Simplicity

There is nothing so strong or safe in an emergency of life
as the simple truth.
—Charles Dickens

The greatest athletes are beautiful to watch because they summon their best abilities at the absolutely necessary moment. Sports fans remember where we were when we saw moments of sheer excellence. These experiences linger in our consciousness because of the high stakes, thrill, and surprise.

Often the athletes seem to be operating in a different world, almost effortlessly, despite being in the midst of an urgent, stressful situation. It's similar to a surgeon handling a tricky procedure, someone defusing a bomb, or a first responder acting in a crisis.

Or astronauts. There's not much margin for error when you're in space, and NASA is rightfully proud of the resourcefulness that its crews have shown in dealing with urgent crises in orbit. When *Apollo 17*'s lunar rover lost a fender, the mission was saved by duct-taping laminated maps. When the International Space Station had a malfunction, the crew used a toothbrush to clean the problem part.[2] This fearlessness in the face of grave danger is a learned behavior. High achievers are inhabiting an optimal consciousness that allows them to relax and perform at their highest capacity.

This is the "state of flow." Here is one description from Mihaly Csikszentmihalyi, the University of Chicago psychologist who coined the term:

> Regardless of the culture, regardless of education or whatever, there are these seven conditions that seem to be there when a person is in flow: There's this focus that, once it becomes intense, leads to a sense of ecstasy, a sense of clarity: you know exactly what you want to do from one moment to the other; you get immediate feedback. You know that what you need to do is possible to do, even though difficult, and your sense of time disappears, you forget yourself, you feel part of something larger. And once the conditions are present, what you are doing becomes worth doing for its own sake.[3]

In state of a flow, time as we know it disappears. Research has shown that flow is achieved through and marked by the following:

- Clear goals

- Concentration

- A loss of feeling of self-consciousness

- Direct and immediate feedback

- Balance between ability and challenge

- A sense of personal control

- Intrinsic reward

- Lack of awareness of bodily needs[4]

Perhaps most of all, flow is the *absorption in the activity and nothing else.* Your focus is utter simplicity. There is no stress, anxiety, or urgency.

"Simple can be harder than complex," Steve Jobs said. "You have to work hard to get your thinking clean to make it simple. But it's worth it in the end because once you get there, you can move mountains."

––––––

URGENCY ROBS TIME and energy from the essential steps on our way to realizing our purpose. Trading urgency for simplicity also means stepping back to focus on your fundamental needs. Can you trade a long laundry list of accomplishments that probably matter more to other people to embrace a few select achievements that have real meaning and significance to you? Think about the last time you gave in to a request because it seemed urgent, and you agreed to take on a time-consuming task. What did you have to give up (time and more) to fulfill this promise? When you consider this cost, it is easier to say no in the future and trade urgency for simplicity.

Simple rituals (mine revolve around staying physical active) are habits that counteract the fear of missing something that is urgent. I've learned to embrace the three core truths that author Greg McKeown describes in his book *Essentialism: The Disciplined Pursuit of Less:* (1) I choose. (2) Only a few things really matter. (3) I can do anything—but not everything.[5]

Getting off the hamster wheel of urgency can take fearlessness. You think you are going to miss something. Part of your ego resists. But what you gain is huge. Ask yourself this simple question: "Is this task essential to my purpose?"[6]

This is an example of how a mission statement is an excellent shield and filter for preserving your time and energy. This pivot from the urgent to the simple will give you control and build your momentum toward greater fearlessness.

We live in small moments in which an automatic yes or no can commit you to a path you don't want. When we fail to focus, we let other people choose for us, and that's a detour from what is most meaningful to us. Stretch your critical moments of decision and action by trading urgency for simplicity.

Simplicity and focus help me fearlessly stay on track. They are powerful responses to the tyranny of the urgent.

Trade Assuming for Inquiring

> *Never cease to stand like curious children*
> *before the great mystery into which we were born.*
> —Albert Einstein

Before a keynote speech, a speaker will get clear on messaging with the leadership of the company whose employees will be in the audience. These preliminary conversations have made a big impression on me because they have enabled me to get inside the heads and hearts of the C-level executives and their teams. The true influencers are sponges for personal growth and learning. They are unafraid to put themselves in the role of a student. They are fear-less about any discomfort that may come from a lack of knowledge or information, and they have no problem admitting ignorance. They choose vulnerability because that's the path to growth. They epitomize poet Robert Frost's definition of *education*: "the ability to listen to almost anything without losing your temper or self-confidence."

This habit stretches critical moments because by nature we are quick to respond to perceived threats. Quick reflexes are the way a species preserves itself. Although the decision to fight or flee can save a life, we seldom face that kind of threat. But our brains are still wired to react that way.

When we decide reactively and not thoughtfully, we are much more likely to be making split-second assumptions about the situation. As an agent, I saw the perils of making such assumptions almost every time a financial planner met with my clients. It wasn't uncommon for an athlete to have, for example, a dad who worked in a shoe store and a mom who juggled three jobs. Was it the celebrity aura that made the planners rush through fancy wealth and investment options? It amazed me that none ever asked my clients about their personal financial goals. They might have discovered that the guy simply wanted his investments to help his parents stop working. Don't assume. Ask!

When we perceive that we have more time to make a decision or take action, we buy ourselves a greater chance of seeing more options, possibilities, and angles. Creativity is more likely to flourish. There's more of a chance to live your new story and distance yourself from the old one that wasn't working for you. For all these reasons, stretching critical moments is so important.

Often we make assumptions because it is easier and less scary than inquiring. What will people think if I ask? When I was 24, I learned the power of trading assuming for inquiring. I was very early in my career as a sports agent, and I needed to replace my little Honda Accord. It had served me well during college and in Atlanta, but it was time to replace it. I wanted a car that was better, which was at odds with my paycheck and budget. Most people in this situation would assume that a nicer car just wasn't possible.

But I knew there was another mindset because I was seeing it demonstrated by veteran agents. The best were rarely defensive, and they were impressively curious about making a deal as favorable as possible. They assumed nothing. They constantly made inquiries, especially as the stakes rose in negotiations.

Recognizing that the purchase of a new car was a major event for me, I wanted to stretch out my process and get the best deal. I didn't want to assume I couldn't have a better car than my budget suggested.

A client, Ray Goff, was the football coach at the University of Georgia, and in small talk I mentioned that I was trying to sell my car. His ears perked up. The car's value was about $8,000. "I'll give you $9,000," he said. Huh?

"You're doing a lot of things right and really getting after it for me," he explained of my performance as an agent. "In fact, I don't even need that car for a few months. Why don't you keep driving it, and I'll go ahead and pay you for it now so you can buy your next car before you hand over the Honda?"

It was a huge break that would not have been possible without letting go of my assumptions about my car prospects. I drove the car as I looked for the best deal, and I stayed inquisitive.

Our top clients often signed deals with local dealerships to get a car for free in exchange for appearances or speeches. I knew these cars often were turned back in by the talent with a few thousand miles on them and then sold off the lot. Bobby Cremins, the head basketball coach at Georgia Tech, had been driving a small Mercedes, the least expensive model. I knew he was upgrading his car and was about to turn it in, so I called the dealership and made a deal to buy it for $8,500. There had been no big windfall or salary increase, just my staying patient and questioning. And I did not assume that the best I could do was what conventional wisdom dictated. Rarely is that true.

Giving up my assumptions led to one generous act after another. When we inquire, we move past fear to find the truth that exists beyond what we can see.

Trade Complacency for Ingenuity

"Impossible" is just a big word thrown around by small men
who find it easier to live in the world they've been given
than to explore the power they have to change it.
—Muhammad Ali

People who are happy with the way things are have less interest in fearlessness. Life is laid out for them in a seemingly straight line, and all they need to do is keep putting one foot in front of the other. Are you stuck in a status quo like that?

When we fail to question the expectations that we mindlessly follow, we end up in a dead end of complacency where fear can fester. We're so used to doing the same old, same old. But what if we change, and there's no security for us right away? What if we fail? What if . . . ?

When you're hungry for something more and better in your life, when you know that your purpose has not been achieved, shaking things up is necessary. This is when you benefit by identifying small moments of complacency and figuring out ways to leverage them. This is the stretching of the moment.

Today I laugh when I think about how my parents modeled this kind of thinking. As a teenage driver, I was backing the family station wagon out of our long driveway. A row of tall thick bushes hugged one side, and I reversed too quickly. A branch caught the passenger side mirror, and I heard the awful sound of metal separating. The mirror dangled by wires as I pulled into the school parking lot.

I knew it wasn't good, and it wasn't going to be better when Dad got involved. He wasn't going to settle for the normal repair at a body shop. I didn't have the money to get it fixed, but he had a creative answer in mind. He wanted to address the problem and send a message.

By the time Dad was done, his roll of duct tape was half its original thickness. The mirror was held in place by the silver gray sticky stuff. It was "fixed," but it sure looked like a mess. It was almost as bad, maybe worse, than leaving it dangling. His message to me: it works now.

Complacency says there is no better way. Ingenuity says there's got to be one. Trade the first for the second, and watch how fearlessness thrives.

My own complacency shocked me after the publication of my previous book, *A Winner's Guide to Negotiating: How Conversation Gets Deals Done*. The book covers five tools of negotiation, and after a keynote I gave, an audience member took me to task. "You missed one!" she said. And she was right. I had not emphasized ingenuity enough in negotiations.

In deal making, you always pay more when you are complacent. You succeed by being creative. Keeping an open mind is also a fundamental behavior of fearless people, not just those who are negotiators.

Success can breed complacency. It's harder to keep pushing when you're ahead. Legendary football coach Nick Saban uses four words to keep striving for his greatest potential. He reminds himself, "You have never arrived."

5

REDIRECTING PERSISTENT BEHAVIORS

Your beliefs become your thoughts.
Your thoughts become your words.
Your words become your actions.
Your actions become your habits.
Your habits become your values.
Your values become your destiny.
—Mahatma Gandhi

O ur habits are powerful engines that create results, and the five trades in this section will help you identify persistent patterns of behavior that work against you—in ways you may not realize—and replace them with rituals that align with your purpose. It's hard work to change from an ingrained behavior to a new habit that will serve as an engine for fearlessness and growth.

You may not even recognize the role of fear in unhelpful behaviors. Most of us are comforted by routines, and change is hard. Those two factors are enough of a deterrent to keep us in a rut. The patterns we seek to identify and change are those that keep us in a state of fear. We have to alter these persistent behaviors, one small moment at a time, to build a fearless mindset.

"To overcome an irrational fear, replace it with a habit," author Seth Godin says. "If you're afraid to write, write a little, every day. Start with an anonymous blog, start with a sentence. Every day, drip, drip, drip, a habit. If you're afraid to speak up, speak up a little, every day. Not to the board of directors, but to someone. A little bit, every day. Habits are more powerful than fears."

Leadership and assertiveness are so important to this process. Not only do we need the desire to achieve persistent patterns of fearlessness but we also need rewards for positive change. We can create a new voice of authority and leadership within us that is calm and assertive, not fearful. That big difference starts by practicing less fear in the small moments.

Trade Routine for Ritual

The NCAA Final Four, the Masters, the NBA Finals—I watched my clients perform in the great pressure cookers in sports, and in those big pressure cookers, I noticed how much routine matters. No athlete, team, or coach gets to this level without consistent patterns of warming up, of preparing for a shot, of running a play—all of those are locked down at this level.

Ritual is more than routine, and it taps into a more powerful sense of identity and purpose beyond the moment. Routines are secure, whereas rituals are centering. Routines can be mindless. Rituals are always mind*ful*.

Rituals are intentional behaviors that often take place away from the spotlight. They are not as much a substitution for routine as an elevation of it. Completing your ritual signals that you are ready for your fullest absorption in your task.

Before I do a keynote, I always do a workout. It's my sure-fire way of cutting through the clutter and keeping my mind sharp. My ritual centers me. What starts as energy often turns to anxiety if we don't channel our emotions positively, and that's when the ritual is a small moment that makes a big difference. When pressure gets big, the best performers think small.[1] A go-to routine helps you practice success; the most effective ritual exterminates fear.

Rituals are not necessarily religious, but they do feel sacred. Without your ritual, you are not quite yourself. A ritual primes you for a state of flow. Notice that *ritual* is singular; I don't suggest you take on multiple rituals. A ritual can be as simple as reading a book such as *The Hunger Games* (that's what LeBron James does before big games[2]).

An effective ritual quiets the noise around you and in your mind. A ritual is different for each person, and it's most effective when focused on what you want to achieve, not what you are trying to avoid. I have been practicing what my friend Tommy Newberry calls the *early morning success ritual* (EMSR).[3] Tommy is a success coach and author who works with many top executives, and the EMSR kick-starts your day with confidence. You write down three specific events or details that would make the day great. Then you write: "Today, I will be. . . ." The EMSR is a small ritual that helps me wake up with optimism and focus, which are necessary for my peak performance.

No matter what habit you choose to make a ritual, calling it a "ritual" instead of a "routine" makes a difference to how you (and maybe others) internalize this action.

A ritual often has an element of visualization. It's powerful to look through your mind's eye to imagine the fulfillment of your purpose and the goals along that path. This deep, deep rehearsal taps into brain circuitry that activates as if you are not just thinking about an action but actually doing it.[4] A ritual that incorporates visualization sets you up for the right mental messaging, so you focus on your optimal outcome.

How you envision success is up to you. For a big league pitcher, it's sitting down the next batter. For you, it might be walking out of the room with a handshake agreement on a deal.

Golfers use a preshot routine before every shot as a psychological ritual. Doing the same thing every time cues the body and mind to execute under pressure. It's as if they can absorb, even enjoy, intense scrutiny and make themselves relax. In this state of flow, they appear fearless, and in a way, they are. Their rituals help them reframe the pressure and almost eliminate it.

Rituals are especially important if your fear threatens to stifle the creative work you are required to do. "[Creative] blocks usually stem from the fear of being judged. If you imagine the world listening, you'll never write a line" said author Erica Jong.[5]

Her ritualized approach is to produce a first draft with the thought that no one will ever read it. The ritual tricks her mind into ignoring her innate fear. Nice trade!

Trade Selfies for Reflection

If you want to be fearless, don't hang out with people who are fearful. Don't go where they go. This fact is the reason for mindful use of social (and all) media, especially what's in your pocket, on your tablet, or wrist. If you are serious about fearlessly pursuing your purpose, you need to take stock of how much time you spend in what stress expert Pamela Rutledge calls "an anxiety hub where people are trying to dispel their anxiety. . . . We see all of this stuff, and we start to feel like the world is a very scary place."[6]

Don't freak out. This trade isn't about giving up social media for good. I use it a ton in my career and to stay connected to people, so I would never say that people should give it up completely. My point is to become aware of how our digital news feeds exaggerate worries and chaos, creating fertile ground for fear to take root.

Social media is a persistent habit. The 1.6 billion users of Facebook and Instagram spend an average of 50 minutes per day on those platforms.[7] Social media is distracting us from reaching our work-related goals too. A 2014 Pew Research Center Study revealed that 56 percent of workers who use digital platforms for work-related purposes agree that this habit distracts from the work they need to do, with 30 percent agreeing strongly.

Feelings of insecurity, inadequacy, envy, and depression can incubate via social media, which, despite its name, can increase isolation at the same time it promotes competition to keep up with what everyone else is doing. The selfie culture, by definition, nurtures narcissism.

A great alternative is reflection, which turns your attention inward to your goals and what your best next steps should be. Reflection is a way of checking in with yourself. Instead of scanning your screen without thought, take Rutledge's advice and set the alarm on your watch or your phone to beep hourly for a moment of reflection.

"Stop and say, 'I'm grateful it's a sunny day. I'm grateful for this cup of coffee. I'm grateful for these nice shoes,'" Rutledge says. "Whatever small thing shifts your brain, you will be shocked at the end of a few days at how great you feel."

Pausing from the selfie culture can be incredibly powerful. In negotiating $500 million in contracts for my sports clients, I learned the power of pausing between the ask and the answer to allow myself to process both emotions and facts, to reflect on the next best move.[8] It sure can be hard to pause when we start drinking from the social media fire hose, but when you are committed to fearlessly pursuing your purpose, the pause for self-reflection can be a huge tool of empowerment.

Reflection, for me, goes hand-in-hand with gratitude. If you struggle with a scarcity mindset (that you never have enough or are never good enough, which is a prevalent message on social media), reflection built around gratitude can help you do a 180. It is claiming the measurement of your life and environment as your own. You're not comparing what you can do, be, or have. That's fearlessness.

Reflection helps ground you in what is here and what matters. This is vital to remember when unexpected events, crises, and loss inevitably occur—the kinds of things social media exaggerates and often makes worse. Reflection can reveal a true path to resilience; it doesn't stop at offering an inspirational quote for you to like. Reflection has been transformative for me, and I have seen it transform others.

Fearlessness is informed by how you look at the world around you. It is shaped by an understanding of your internal landscape. Reflection is that shift to your own needs and desires amid the recognition that time is passing—and with it, opportunities big and small. Without this sort of reality check, it's awfully easy to succumb to mindless surfing.

In the sport of competitive gymnastics, fear can lead to poor performance and sliding self-confidence. It even causes some young gymnasts to quit the sport entirely. One research study found that a common and effective antidote to this fear was replacing negative thoughts ("I'm scared" or "I can't do this") with a cue such as "Just do it."[9] The cue effectively puts the gymnast's body on autopilot to attempt the exercise or routine.

You don't have to be a gymnast to adopt a consistent practice of trading external fears for confident self-talk. You do need to commit to reflection to determine the thought patterns and messages you are giving yourself that are keeping you in fear. The best part about this habit is that you can practice it anytime through visualization. Fearlessness takes focus, one moment of reflection at a time.

Trade Grudges for Gratitude

> *Every moment is a moment of grace.*
> —Elie Wiesel

The world heard these powerful words when Elie Wiesel accepted his Nobel Peace Prize in 1986. As a boy he had survived the Buchenwald concentration camp, and American soldiers were his heroes. He felt gratitude for them the rest of his life. "Gratitude is a word that I cherish," he said in 1999.[10] "Gratitude is what defines the humanity of the human being."

To endure the horrors of Nazi Germany and to ultimately lead a life of inspiration and courage, as an author and speaker, he made a powerful choice: he would build a wonderful life from the persecution he had suffered because it had given him tremendous insights into what it means to be human. He had every reason to remain in anger and bitterness, but he made a different choice. While acknowledging what had happened, he went forward in life through a lens of gratitude, becoming a role model for generations.

That's fearlessness.

I share his story as an extreme example of the power of choosing gratitude. Our daily lives cannot be compared to the atrocities of the Holocaust, but we certainly can draw inspiration from the lessons of history to live our best lives today.

We don't exert ultimate control over our lives. Unfortunate and unplanned events happen to us on our way to achieving our goals. What story do you tell yourself in the small moments when you feel under personal attack? Do you say, "This always happens to me"? Or "Why me?"

This mindset can be persistent and pernicious. It goes beyond the glass-half-empty outlook. It is a default setting that automatically puts you in a defensive mode. The victim mindset is rooted in fear, excuses, and the perception that control is outside of yourself. It takes courage to own your life, your actions, your mistakes and failures.

In 2009, I experienced a relevant moment with one of my ballplayers. Jeff Francoeur was living his dream playing for the Atlanta Braves, his hometown team. Four years after an amazing rookie start, Francoeur was battling a slump. One evening he called me upset on his way home from the ballpark.

Bobby Cox, the Braves' manager, whom the players loved, had summoned Francoeur into his office to break the news: the Braves had traded him to the New York Mets.

Francoeur was devastated. He was deeply disappointed in himself personally, in himself as a teammate, and in every way that you can imagine someone would feel if he or she were deposed from the pinnacle he or she had dreamed about his or her entire life.

Francoeur was at a fragile point, and his choice of how to face this bad news started that night. Would he get wrapped up in fear and hold a big grudge against the Braves? That kind of thinking does motivate some players.

I wanted to see him go in a more positive direction. We talked about the gift that comes from a fresh start. I tried to help him look forward, not back. Francoeur decided to take the high road.

He said good-bye to the team, acknowledging how special it was to have played for them.[11] "I've had nothing but great experiences," Francoeur said. "Nobody can ever take that away from me." He expressed his anticipation of the challenge of playing in New York, and he put negativity aside as he headed north.

When he got to the Mets' clubhouse, he stayed open to finding something good for himself. He enjoyed the amazing clubhouse meals prepared by a mother-daughter duo. He got a fresh start at the plate and in the field. By deciding not to carry a grudge, he ultimately wound his way through a couple of Major League teams and, in 2016, back to the Braves.[12]

Grudges start with "you" and "they" language. Shifting from this mindset begins when you focus on "I" and "me." You begin to own what has happened, to see your role in it and your options. The more quickly you can make this pivot, the more quickly you can make the best of it. That's where gratitude comes in.

Sonia Thompson is a reinventor who faced many obstacles when she founded TRY Business School, where she helps business owners find the right strategy and mindset to build and grow their businesses. A year after she had traded the security of corporate life for the uncertainty of entrepreneurship, a crisis hit her:

> I got sick and ended up in the hospital. My recovery took months, and I wasn't able to work during that time. When the dust settled, I was left with a mountain of debt.

That experience and its aftermath was the realization
of my worst fears coming true when it came to being an
entrepreneur. I went through a range of emotions and felt
like a failure. I wondered why this happened to me.

That's a perfect description of a victim mindset. We've all
been there. Who hasn't said the words, "Why me?" Thompson
knew that she didn't want to remain a victim. She kept trying to
find a way forward:

Eventually, I landed in a place of thankfulness. I realized
how blessed I was in spite of a few difficulties. I was thankful that I knew that even though life may decide to hit you
with a truck, it doesn't have to be the end of you or your
dreams. It's only the end of the story if you let it be.

At the end of that emotional roller coaster, I felt powerful. And the lessons I've learned throughout this journey
have transformed the way I view challenges in my business and my ability to overcome them.

So now, if things don't go quite the way I want, I recognize that I have the power to make them different. All I
have to do is identify the root cause of the issue, seek out
solutions, implement the ones that are right for me, and
make adjustments as I get new information. The changes
may not come instantaneously, but if I'm diligent with my
plan of action, I will see positive change.

Her story affirms this conclusion: the antidote to victim-
hood is gratitude. Here's my related ritual. Every morning I write
down three things I am grateful for and three things that would
make the day great. The act of writing solidifies my personal

mission statement and emphasizes the responsibility I have to my decisions and actions. It's one thing to think that the sky is beautiful on a morning walk, but it becomes even more real and personal when I put my gratitude for that in words on paper. A tool like *The Five Minute Journal* makes it easy to stick to this simple act as a daily ritual.

Those words reflect small moments that foretell a big outcome. Thankfulness refreshes my best perspective on the things that happen that I don't control.

When we start with gratitude in small moments, we can easily turn to what our response can be instead of focusing on fear and blame for what others might have done or not done. Gratitude opens the way to fearlessness.

Trade Gossip for Influence

Fearlessness doesn't happen in a vacuum. It requires a great deal of trust in yourself. Some people call this "confidence", the belief that you can do what you tell yourself is possible. Trust is so important that it may be impossible to achieve fearlessness without it.

One of the most powerful forces that can instantly tear down trust is gossip. When you gossip, you break down boundaries of trust on several fundamental levels. If gossip is a persistent habit for you, my goal is to help you see how detrimental this is to living your fullest purpose.

Let's take a typical scenario:

Person A, who trusts you, shares a confidence.

You share that information with Person B, and it becomes gossip. It's not your story to tell. In this small moment, you have betrayed Person A and proved to Person B that you are someone who doesn't value trust. Perhaps worst of all, you have proven *to yourself* that you are untrustworthy.

Whether you start it or take part in it, gossip is a lose-lose-lose situation. Trust is "not just about the fact you hold my confidences, but in our relationship you acknowledge confidentiality," says author and researcher Brené Brown.[13] She points out that we often trade information as gossip because we want to "hot-wire" our relationship with Person B. Or we recognize Person A as a dislikable third party, and we share gossip to create "common enemy intimacy." The result is not real trust; true intimacy can't be built on hating the same people.

Gossip, in my experience, comes from a mindset of false competition in which we see ourselves as independent individuals who don't or shouldn't need to rely on anyone else. When we are Lone Rangers, other people don't matter as much, and it's easier to cut them down in our words or actions. Those small moments of gossip chip away at our influence in the lives of those we hold closest. We're not tearing other people down. We are tearing ourselves down.

Trust is built in small moments when we make the choice to build or betray. Brown pointed to the work of noted marriage therapist John Gottmann, who for decades has studied how and why couples stay together. His research has noted that over time, the choice not to connect in the small moments results in a big outcome: emotional betrayal.[14]

Turns out the high road is paved with wonderful brain hormones. Choosing to connect positively—instead of giving in to the impulse of selfishness, gossip, or criticism—releases oxytocin, which makes us feel bonded. We are part of something bigger, and from this base we feel confident and fearless. Those closest to us have our backs.

Another reason for gossip can be insecurity and a lack of attention.[15] If you are baited into gossip by someone with these issues, you need to exert your influence for good. Try politely and professionally saying, "Why are you sharing this information with me?" Directly confronting the gossip takes some satisfaction out of it. Asking for facts and the reasoning behind the gossip can also stop it.

As powerful as gossip is, trading it away opens up a huge amount of positive space to practice fearlessness. We can access so many moments to connect and have influence with the people in our lives.

Influence is leveraging the difference we can make in our daily interactions in those small moments. We matter when we connect to our purpose and to those who trust us and whom we trust. Most people don't recognize or tap this power to its potential.

Too often, we choose gossip as a toxic way to grab power and instill fear in others. I experienced this in an office environment, and maybe you have too. A supervisor would usher me into his office, close the door, and dish on my colleagues about poorly executed projects, client relationships, or their inability to sell.

For various personal and professional reasons, he criticized everyone but me. His words created a false sense of connection, that I would be OK as long as he was happy.

Of course, I figured out that this treatment was far from special: he was doing this to everyone! He could have leveraged that opportunity to provide mentorship or otherwise positively influence us and our morale. Instead, he made the opposite decision. The main takeaway that stuck with me is how to never manage people that way.

Gossip drives a wedge between people because when they no longer trust you, fear can grow. Trust is the backbone of fearlessness. With trust comes influence. The choice in the small moments to connect or betray reveals your character and determines the amount of trust that others put in you.

Make each moment—in the spotlight or not—count toward your purpose and best self.

Trade Complacency for Ownership

As a teenage tennis player, I hit a frustrating plateau. I needed to be more aggressive. Even younger players were more fearless in going to the net and finishing the point.

Growing up in Michigan, I was a long way from any ocean when my coach taught me the "sharks game." I'll never forget the heat of humiliation rising in me as he explained this seemingly childish game to me.

"Behind the baseline are sharks in the ocean! If you step behind the line during this point, you will lose the point and get eaten by sharks!"

To avoid stepping behind the line and thereby win the point, I had to move to the net and hit a shot that would take my opponent off balance. These moments formed a powerful realization that I could literally step toward what I wanted in life—or I could wait and let it come to me. When I waited for something to come to me, sometimes someone else stepped in and I lost my chance to achieve what I wanted. I realized that being my best self was about cutting off the angle—taking the meaningful action now instead of later.

As every graduating college student can attest, life comes at you fast when the real world beckons. After four years at Michigan State University, it was time for my next chapter.

Staying in East Lansing was a safe and tempting option. I would have the continued support of my family and friends. I had enough relationships there that I could find a job and be comfortable. But what I really wanted to pursue was a career in the sports industry, and I had to be realistic. That opportunity wasn't going to land in my lap in East Lansing.

Fresh out of school, it was time for me to take ownership of my life, which before that moment had always unfolded in a steady, predictable fashion without much intention on my part. This step would be different. I sat on the living room floor of my parents' house with my two best friends. Between us, we spread out a huge map of the United States.

Where would I start my next chapter? The map, filled with places I'd never been before, was at once exhilarating and terrifying. After much discussion, I settled on my choice.

A red pushpin marked the spot: Atlanta, Georgia.

I chose Atlanta because it was ripe for opportunity in the sports space. The Super Bowl and the Olympics were both coming to the city. And to further solidify my choice, I had a friend living there who had offered up a spot on her couch until I could land on my feet.

With $2,000 in my pocket, I packed up my Honda Accord and kissed my parents good-bye. Not many tears were shed because they were both pretty certain I'd be headed back up 75 North when my money ran out.

In my 12-hour journey south, I drew on lessons from the sharks game. Before I learned to go to the net, why had I felt comfortable on the baseline? I had a fear of looking like I didn't know what I was doing. A real fear that I did not *belong* near the net. The sharks game taught me to claim my power and place. No one could give that to me.

I felt comfortable on the baseline partly because I feared I did not *belong* near the net. But imagining the sharks near the baseline had forced me to learn that by cutting the angle, I got to the ball faster. Every I time had executed it during a match, I had become a better player. Going for it taught me that with risk also came reward.

Now it was time to apply that tennis lesson to life. If I wanted to land a job in such a competitive industry, I had to make it happen myself. I had to cut off the angle and go for it.

That's exactly what I did. Knowing I needed to stretch my money, I negotiated a deal with a nearby apartment complex to waive my rent. How? I knew there was a position as a tennis pro opening up at the complex, so I approached the manager of the complex and inquired about teaching at the property. I found ways to add value so that I could leverage the position for free rent. I persuaded a neighborhood pizza shop in Atlanta to provide discounted pizzas for residents and free pizzas for our clinics. I leaned on my long-term relationship with Wilson Sporting Goods to provide freebies such as gear and rackets for residents who participated in the tennis clinics. I even wrote tennis tips for the resident newsletter. All these little gestures turned into nine years of living rent free in that apartment complex. Small moments, big outcomes!

Eventually all those small moments added up, and I landed my dream job in sports. But what got me to that point was learning to trade complacency for ownership. Just as my tennis coach had taught me, great things happen when we anticipate and take a calculated risk to go for it.

Fearing less comes from choosing to take ownership of your life—what matters to you, your purpose in life. Don't wait on the baseline for life to come at you. Step forward and make it happen. Trade complacency for ownership, and tap into your fearlessness.

6

REFRAMING BAD NEWS

The difference between stumbling blocks and
stepping-stones is how you use them.
—Anonymous

Not long ago I met with the top leadership of a thriving entertainment and restaurant company. Profits were climbing almost 10 percent annually. Growth over time had been dramatic. The leaders were crystal clear about the factors they could or could not control. They were always prepared, whether the news was good or bad.

Fearlessness is a whole lot easier when things are going well. But what about when life (inevitably) delivers disappointment? This is when fear can take hold. What we thought was a sure thing didn't happen. What's our next move? What if we can't recover?

Being fearless is becoming comfortable with moments that produce the opposite result from what we had hoped. Fearlessness hinges on understanding that even in the midst of bad news, we still can control our attitudes and reactions.

Fearless people accept that bad news will come; we're human and things happen. We don't have to panic. We can learn and grow. In that way, we can reframe bad news.

Bad news tests our purpose. Is it elastic enough to accommodate moments of disappointment and find the lessons that are offered?

The trades in this chapter are very important for anyone who is taking a risk. The more you put yourself out there, the more you risk disappointment. These are the stakes of vulnerability. You are forced to come to terms with being at a point where you may feel most fearful and your purpose depends on your embracing fearlessness.

Practicing these five trades will help you become confident that you are going to take every lemon and make your own kick-ass lemonade. When bad news unfolds, you will be able to manage the situation because you will have practiced controlling what you can in the small moments. You will be able not only to stay on course during bad news but to reframe it so that something positive comes out of it.

Trade Rejection for Education

You have rejection, and you have to learn how to deal with that and how to get up the next day and go on with it.
—Taylor Swift

Every author faces rejection letters, and I've received plenty—so many from publishers regarding my first book that I considered using them for wallpaper. My first manuscript was 40,000 words of advice that I hoped would help people get their dream job. The idea for the book came from rejection: I couldn't meet individually with all the young people who wanted to pick my brain and land their dream job (usually in sports). When I saw someone fumble away an opportunity for a dream job, my heart broke. The book, which I wrote soon after my twins and their older sister were born 12 and a half months apart, offered a one-stop education for young adults who were constantly coming to me for advice.

Despite the rejections, I stuck with the project. I kept educating myself on publishing requirements. Finally my persistence broke the cycle, and my first published book, *The 5 Best Tools to Find Your Dream Career*, helped me reach and educate thousands seeking jobs that offered them fulfillment and not just a paycheck.

When you are strong in your purpose, failure and fear become speed bumps, not roadblocks. These remind us of how we don't want to feel, and we don't have to be stuck in the bad news of rejection. We can learn from these moments so that we can pivot better the next time. Rejection is such a common form of bad news. Even people who are super successful at very intense jobs and high-pressure careers fear rejection. If you are a high achiever, or you aspire to that level, trading rejection for education is extremely relevant to your success.

As a sports agent, I learned to love rejection. That may sound ridiculous, but it's true.

Because there are so many more agents than there are athletes, I was fishing from a very crowded shore. Trying to get a foothold of any kind was hard because lasting relationships were few and often formidable.

Sometimes I would meet with athletes who already had agents and were happy. The wife of one athlete was adamant about sticking with their agent. I took the rejection as a challenge to become as educated as possible about their needs, fears, resources, and limitations. I sought to use my education about their needs to better educate them because I was convinced they did not know what they were missing. I became sure that they thought they were happy because they did not know they could be happier. Eventually, my firm won him over.

In negotiating, I learned quickly that a "no" isn't always what it sounds like. What else can "no" mean? It can mean "maybe," "not now," or "try again. "No" doesn't have to be personal, and a single "no" does not predict "no" forever. "No" is simply feedback.

When I hear "no," I try to sidestep any defensiveness on my part and quickly get curious. "Tell me more," I might say. I stay open and hopeful that the person rejecting me will take the next step and educate me.

The key to fearlessness is simply staying in the game, to continue the conversation and not let post-rejection feelings stop you. "What do you do when life tells you no?" Seattle Seahawks quarterback Russell Wilson asked in his commencement speech at the University of Wisconsin.[1] "When life tells you no, find a way to keep things in perspective. That doesn't make the painful moments any less painful. But it does mean you don't have to live forever in the pain. You don't have to live forever in that no. Because if you know what you're capable of, if you're always prepared, and you keep things in perspective, then life has a way of turning a no into a yes."

Whenever appropriate, treat a "no" more like a yellow light than a red light and keep pursuing your purpose. The more quickly you make this trade, the sooner you can absorb key information.

This is what I have learned from making this trade countless times over my career: Rejection doesn't necessarily mean the end of a relationship. Sometimes rejection is actually a hidden gift.[2] If you can reframe a "no" into a "not now," you remain open. When your mind is more open and optimistic, fear has less chance to grow.

It's easier to make this trade when you have purpose and vision that elevates you from worrying about anyone else. How do you define happiness? Your "better" and "best" are up to you. Your purpose offers a road map for educating others (by word or action) about what you are learning as you grow. As you strive for more education related to your purpose, you're also learning to embrace new knowledge and allowing it to take up space inside you. There's less room for fear to take root.

Sales is just one field where this applies. When you are in an industry that offers a very short window of time to capitalize on (like professional sports offers for performers), it's much more common to face pressure and rejection. This trade is really about rejecting the rejection. Pursuing knowledge (instead of staying mired in rejection) is an act of fearlessness that helps create momentum and confidence. It is how we learn that we can make the world better even if others don't see us and our gifts that way.

When you're faced with "no," don't make bad news worse. Take it as an opportunity to practice fearlessly educating yourself and preparing yourself to educate others.

Trade Envy for Attentiveness

Today Lee Katz is the chairperson of GGG Partners, one of the leading turnaround firms in the country. But in 1964 he was just a 13-year-old making peanuts and hawking snacks to sports fans at Georgia Tech football games. He would sell each bag for 10 cents and get a token for profit. The big money was in the competition with his fellow peanut sellers. The person who sold the most bags daily—who turned in the most tokens—earned a $20 bonus. Lee wanted those big bucks.

"There was no second or third place. There was only number one," Katz explained.[3] He could have been envious and left it at that. But he got busy working on the strategy to achieve his goal.

Katz identified the top sellers and paid attention when they compared tokens throughout the day. He got a good estimate of how many tokens he needed for a comfortable winning margin. Getting those was easy. He simply bought enough extra bags of peanuts from himself.[4]

From his early experience hawking peanuts, the big outcomes for Katz ultimately were attaining degrees in industrial engineering and law and thriving as a leader who turns around struggling companies. He now specializes in financial restructuring, bankruptcy restructuring, asset liquidations, bond restructuring, and corporate downsizing. He's constantly sizing up what he has to work with and cutting deals.

Katz's story shows how we face choices in pursuing what we desire. How do you deal with something you want but don't have or can't have right now? Do you get stuck in wishful thinking? Does this dead end distract you from taking productive actions toward your purpose?

Envy works like that, especially in competition, because chances are someone is going to be ahead of you. It is defined as a feeling of discontented or resentful longing aroused by someone else's possessions, qualities, or luck. That person is taking control over your frame of mind and quality of life. Very quickly envy can lead to misery and worry. Envy and jealousy lead to fear of losing what you already have. Envy is not going to help you go anywhere; instead, it's going to keep you from where you need to go.

At one of my tennis matches, my dad listened as his friend complimented him on my brother Johnny's being accepted into "Top Gun" school as a Navy pilot and for Johnny's twin, Jimmy, being at the top of his class at the Air Force Academy.

"Boy, Ken, look at this with your daughter playing tennis and your sons doing so well," the friend said. "You're so lucky."

Dad stared him down.

"This has absolutely nothing to do with luck," Dad said flatly.

He could quickly draw that distinction because to him, success came from fearlessly taking care of the small things in life, small things that require close attention. My parents' support of my desire to play tennis at a high level helped me see how important it is to trade envy for attentiveness.

Growing up watching local stars such as Lindsay Davenport and Todd Martin, I wanted to be as accomplished as they were. My coach also worked with Todd Martin, who wasn't supposed to be as good as he actually was on the court. I wanted to be an overachiever like that.

"If you want to play like a champ," my coach said, "you need to look like a champ. Pay attention to how you look. Tuck your shirt in."

I stopped looking at Martin, Davenport, and others, and I began looking hard at myself. Really looking. It wasn't about copying them but identifying what I needed to work on myself. Attentiveness was about seeing what I could do to achieve my unique purpose and not getting stuck wishing I had someone else's success. My coach taught me that *where you direct your attention is where you place your energy*, and that understanding helped me decide where to put my focus.

This lesson kept repeating itself as I developed my awareness of small moments that make a difference. It resonated at a recent leadership conference called Leadercast from speaker Nick Saban, the football coach at the University of Alabama.[5] Surprisingly, his team doesn't hear him talk about winning. Instead, Saban talks about process. About being in the moment. About focusing on what you can control. "Be where your feet are now," is one of his favorite expressions. He says success is a result of constantly asking ourselves, "What's important now?" Great acronym too: WIN.

Envy is a survival mindset; attentiveness is a creation mindset. Becoming attentive means working on what you uniquely can bring to the world. Why not lean into the behaviors that give us the best opportunity for success? The highest performers understand that minding these small habits and little moments—even the simple choice to tuck in a shirt—can lead to big outcomes.

Tucking in my shirt helped me grasp the power of attentiveness. It was one small moment en route to my competitive pinnacle: playing Division I tennis. Small acts of fearlessness helped me get there.

In small moments when you feel envy rise, recognize it as bad news. Try attentiveness instead. It works.

Trade What Now for What If

> *The moments when life tells you yes aren't the ones*
> *that define you. The moments that really matter*
> *are the moments when life tells you no.*
> —Russell Wilson, NFL quarterback

Whether you are in business or sports or another field, going from good to great is one of the hardest tasks anyone can attempt.

And the harder the challenge, the more likely you will encounter bad news, and the more important it is to try to make the best of bad news.

Russell Wilson received some bad news early in his football career at North Carolina State University.[6] His dream had been to play quarterback, but as his first college season approached, his coach reassigned him to a defensive position.

In that *what now* moment, Wilson dug down. He decided that he couldn't simply go along with his coach's decision without expressing his belief in his ability to play quarterback and deliver for the team. What if he could persuade his coach to change his mind and give him a chance? With deep conviction in his ability and with a sense of peace no matter the outcome, he decided to approach his coach fearlessly. "I'm going to be your starting quarterback," Wilson proclaimed at one point during their meeting. The bold move and Wilson's intense belief in himself worked, and three days later he was named the starting quarterback. He built a reputation for fearless style, inspirational leadership, and intense preparation.

Then came his final season. Although he had already graduated early, Wilson had one year of football eligibility remaining, and he decided to return to the team for his final season, with his dream of reaching the pros on the horizon. The coach delivered some tough words: "Listen, son, you're never going to play in the National Football League. You're too small. There's no chance. You got no shot. Give it up."

Again, Wilson faced a *what now* situation: "This was everything I had worked for. And now it was completely gone. If I wanted to follow my dream, I had to leave.... I had no idea if I would get a second chance somewhere else."

Because he had performed so well in his dream position, his *what now* situation caught the attention of rival coaches. They began asking, "*What if* Wilson could play for them instead?" He had multiple offers from great teams, transferred to the University of Wisconsin for his final year, set a college passing record, and led his team to the Rose Bowl title. The Seattle Seahawks signed him, and he led them to victory in the 2013 Super Bowl. "In the end, what had started out as the biggest no of my career became the biggest yes of my career," he said.

Trading *what now* for *what if* can be so powerful because it moves you from the emotion of bad news to a solution-oriented frame of mind, which is a place of fearlessness.

What now is the voice of pessimism, and that negativity can breed fear. You have a choice to feed it or refocus on *what if*.

"*What if* I try something new in the face of this challenge?" "*What if* this closed door will open another passage that I hadn't considered?"

"*What if* this bad news is really an opportunity for greater growth?" "*What if* this bad news is simply an obstacle like the ones that all successful people encounter and deal with on their way to a goal?" "*What if* this bad news is something I will look back on as benefiting me, and I can go ahead and look at it that way?"

Other creative and successful people have used this thinking. Actor Drew Barrymore used to struggle with her body image, telling herself she could not wear sleeveless or strapless clothing. "All of a sudden I was like, 'What if I just didn't send such negative messages to my brain and said, wear it and enjoy it?'" Now she is more comfortable in her clothes and in her skin.

"When we reassure the voice in our head by rationally reminding it of everything that will go right, we actually reinforce it," says author and marketing guru Seth Godin.[7] "Life without fear doesn't last very long—you'll be run over by a bus or a boss—before you know it. The fearless person, on the other hand, sees the world as it is—fear included—and then makes smart—and brave—decisions."

What if drives you to become fearless, keeping you focused away from the *what now* thinkers. At the core, this trade is very much like trading defensiveness for curiosity. It is the expression of a mindset that belongs to a lifelong learner. We can apply that thinking to our small decisions, choosing a mindset of possibility in the moment so that it becomes a ritual that propels us to our purpose.

This trade is a powerful shift into realizing what life holds for us when we look at events differently. The more we can do this in the small moments, the more we position ourselves for greater outcomes. It takes fearing less to start thinking this way, and thinking this way builds great fearlessness over time.

Trade Short-Term Pain for Long-Term Growth

> *The only way you are going to have success*
> *is to have lots of failures first.*
> —Sergey Brin, cofounder of Google

Our bodies teach us that pain can be good news in the process of growth. That's the pivot that fearless achievers in business and sports make in small moments of pain, to recognize and welcome these moments as stepping-stones to long-term growth.

A great example of this ability to trade pain for growth is the story of Jeff Francoeur and Brian McCann.

Francoeur burst into Major League Baseball as a rookie phenomenon and the hometown darling of the Atlanta Braves. He had so much athletic talent that he gave up a football scholarship to Clemson. He had movie star looks too.

But the main thing you need to know was that Francoeur had not suffered much failure along the way. He was, as *Sports Illustrated* called its cover boy, "The Natural." Because I was his agent, I could see clearly that Francoeur had enjoyed growth without a lot of struggle. People gave him credit for making his success look almost effortless.

Especially compared to Brian McCann. Brian McCann had grown up with Francoeur in the same county in suburban Atlanta. McCann faced bad news whenever he was compared to Francoeur: he didn't have the natural talent, charm, or charisma. Even the position he played, catcher, covered him up.

McCann had to work hard. He knew what struggling was. He learned to value the small moments of opportunity to work into the pain. He took care of these, and incrementally he began to see his value rise.

Fast-forward to the big leagues. Things changed. Francoeur struggled at the plate. Pitchers figured him out, and he didn't cope well because he had never experienced anything like this.

"I just was going off raw talent," Francoeur said. "But after a while, you have to be able to hone it and do something, and at that point, I wasn't able to. For two to three years, it was great and it all worked, and then I didn't know how to handle the failure when it happened."[8]

Meanwhile, McCann stayed steady. He was a reliable hitter with stamina for the season. The two were acting out a version of the tortoise and hare fable. McCann would never have the pure athleticism of his peer, and no one would call him a stud. What he did have was a commitment to the process of whittling down his mistakes and taking advantage of the small moments.

Baseball's long season and 162 games mean that the small moments really add up. The player with the big play may be the hero, but if he's prone to injury and on the disabled list for a month, that heroism isn't accounting for much more than memories. In baseball and life, the long haul is made up of all the little moments. The teams that make it to the World Series have taken care of more of the little moments than any of their competitors. They have clarity and purpose that help sustain them through the pain and allow growth to happen.

When we trade short-term pain for long-term growth, we build resilience and the ability to recover from adversity. We reverse our natural inclination to fear pain and failure, accepting that both help us grow.

Take muscles, for example. We work out, and we know we are going to be sore. The more and harder we work out, the more sore we are going to be. That's our muscles telling us they are growing. They are getting stronger.

"The last three or four reps is what makes the muscle grow," former professional bodybuilder Arnold Schwarzenegger has said. "This area of pain divides the champion from someone else who is not a champion. That's what most people lack, having the guts to go on and just say they'll go through the pain no matter what happens."

Muscles won't grow without discomfort; that's why growing pains are real. The joints of a teenager who is rapidly getting taller and bigger are going to hurt. Look at the small (and sometimes big) moments of short-term pain and see the positive long-term outcome.

"Fearlessness is like a muscle," media mogul Arianna Huffington says in her book *On Becoming Fearless*. "I know from my own life that the more I exercise it, the more natural it becomes to not let my fears run me."

As time goes by, the pain of growth fades even more, and the joy of our more present memories becomes greater. When we choose to focus on growth in the small moments of pain, the big outcome is leaving the fear behind. Ultimately we are so much bigger than our bad news.

Trade Mistakes for Advancement

Vera Bradley Designs, the wildly popular Fort Wayne–based producer of handbags, luggage, and other accessories, is known for its high-quality quilted-cotton accessories in stylish patterns and vibrant hues.

The impetus for the company came about when cofounders Patricia R. Miller and Barbara Bradley Baekgaard noticed the dull-colored luggage of passengers in the Atlanta airport during a layover. Entrepreneurs at heart, they thought aloud: "Wouldn't women love to have luggage that was both functional and feminine?"

Within weeks, the longtime friends and business partners had put together a business plan and pooled the resources necessary to launch a company capable of manufacturing unique handbags and luggage. As in many start-ups, there wasn't much margin for error. So when an order arrived with a large quantity of the wrong-sized zipper, they could have lost valuable time waiting for a new order. Instead, they chose to "turn lemons into lemonade," as Miller put it.

"We were in our infancy as a company, and it was just the two of us at the time," Miller recalled.[9] "Instead of treating it as some sort of massive mistake, we looked at each other and thought, 'Why not design an attaché utilizing this zipper size instead?' It ended up being a top seller."

In the midst of a seemingly costly mistake, Miller and Baekgaard recognized the hidden opportunity to create something different and unique.

The vision and growth mindset of these two brilliant business minds launched the company onto a path of continued success and eventually took the company public (Nasdaq: VRA). Great leaders stay creative and look for opportunities for growth, regardless of the circumstances.

Trade Panic for Cooperation

Even when bad news gives you every reason to panic, you have a choice. We've seen over and over that "regular" people are capable of great acts of fearlessness in a crisis, even the kind that makes headlines.

I love the story about Sully, the pilot who in 2009 landed his plane in the Hudson River and saved the lives of all 155 passengers and crew. It's a perfect example of this mindset. After birds knocked out the engines of his American Airlines jet, Chesley "Sully" Sullenberger had only brief minutes to figure out what to do. How did he skillfully manage a water landing in the waters off Manhattan with no loss of life?

In one of his first lengthy interviews after his act of heroism, Sullenberger said everything turned on a wordless understanding between the people who needed to be in place to do their specific jobs: the first responders on the ground, the flight crew that calmed the passengers and helped them brace for impact, and mostly him and his first officer, Jeff Skiles:

> Our cooperation was done largely by observing the other and not communicating directly because of the extreme time pressure. Jeff and I worked together seamlessly and very efficiently, very quickly, without directly verbalizing a lot of issues. We were observing the same things, we had

the same perceptions, and it was clear to me that he was hearing what I was saying to Air Traffic Control on the radio. He was observing my actions, and I was observing his, and it was immediately obvious to me that his understanding of the situation was the same as mine, and that he was quickly and efficiently taking the steps to do his part. . . .

I felt it was like the best of both worlds. I could use my experience, I could look out the window and make a decision about where we were going to go, while he was continuing his effort to restart the engines and hoping that we wouldn't have to land someplace other than a runway. He was valiantly trying until the last moment to get the engines started again.[10]

For Sullenberger, the fearless cooperation that preceded the moment of impact in the Hudson and the successful outcome were the result of a lifetime of preparation in thousands of other small moments:

The way I describe this whole experience . . . is that everything I had done in my career had in some way been a preparation for that moment. There were probably some things that were more important than others or that applied more directly. But I felt like everything I'd done in some way contributed to the outcome—of course, along with [the actions of] my first officer and the flight attendant crew, the cooperative behavior of the passengers during the evacuation, and the prompt and efficient response of the first responders in New York.

That's truly the mindset of someone who makes the best of bad news. Every challenge had prepared him for this moment.

My twin brothers are pilots, and their training involved working through situations in which, for example, the engines were shut off. They had to replace panic with cooperation— working together with the crew to move forward, not back, with whatever resources were at hand.

If you respond to little moments with cooperation, you build a mindset where there is no place to fear and no room for panic. You're prepared to turn any bad news into a big and positive outcome.

SHIFTING TOXIC THINKING

As a single footstep will not make a path on the earth,
so a single thought will not make a pathway in the mind.
To make a deep physical path, we walk again and again.
To make a deep mental path, we must think over and over
the kind of thoughts we wish to dominate our lives.
—Henry David Thoreau

Fear separates winners and losers at the negotiating table, as I observed for two decades as a sports agent. Fear arises from toxic thinking, so if you can shift those thoughts, you set yourself up for fearlessness.

Case in point: negotiating for salary. A salary.com survey of almost 2,000 workers found nearly one-fifth never negotiated after they were offered a job, and more than three-quarters of respondents said they regretted not doing so.[1]

They were held back by toxic thinking: too worried about losing the job offer, doubting their ability to ask, not feeling like it, and so on. Other answers participants provided included "I don't want to come across as greedy" and "It never seems to make a difference anyway."

And yet by not negotiating, they left money on the table. Their toxic thinking kept them from representing their value and seeking fair compensation. The cost of not negotiating can be more than $500,000 by the time an employee is age 60.[2] That's the price of this mistaken mentality.

Toxic thinking isn't glass-half-empty pessimism. It's subtler and can manifest in a fixed mindset, perfectionism, acceptance of mediocrity, worry, and magical thinking. Recognizing those negative patterns is the first step to replacing them with habits that lead to fearlessness.

Getting out of toxic thinking can be as simple as extending the benefit of the doubt. Think of the new patterns in this chapter as sharp garden tools for tackling the weeds in your head, those toxic thoughts. Some of them have pretty deep roots, and it will take time and work to nurture a healthier mental landscape.

Some people survive by operating against worst-case scenarios. But to thrive and become fearless, you must replace this kind of toxic thinking. With these trades, you will plant habits that drive your best outcomes.

Trade the Status Quo for Creativity

When I needed a car as a teenager, my parents bought me a big ugly beat-up station wagon. Most of my friends drove better cars by far. But my dad knew that heavy clunker would keep me safe driving in Michigan's ice and snow (his theory was that the big front on the car would protect me if I ever slid into a tree or, God forbid, another car).

So what if it didn't look great? It got me where I needed to go. It got the job done.

When cell phones and their car antennas became popular, our family budget couldn't afford such a luxury. One day I came home to see a new addition to my station wagon: an antenna on the left back window. My heart leaped at the thought of a cell phone. I ran to the car to check it out.

Inside, under the stereo, was a cell phone! I picked it up, but something was very wrong. It was plastic. Totally fake. So was the antenna taped to the back window.

"Dad? Seriously?" I said when I walked into the house.

"I got you a cell phone," he said, smiling. Yeah, the best decoy a few dollars could buy, I thought.

And yet it worked. Not long after, I was at a stoplight, and I looked over at a guy staring at me, but I didn't freak out. I just picked up my plastic cell phone.

The whole setup was Dad's sense of humor coming through. It was also his creativity. Creativity was his way of addressing his instinctive fear for my safety. That's such a vulnerable point, isn't it? Our default setting is programmed to do everything we can to give our children and our significant others every chance to stay healthy and thrive. But we can't control what happens to them—no one can!

My dad was always bucking the status quo, which keeps everyone in place and erases doubt about doing the right thing. If you're keeping up with the Joneses, you don't have to think for yourself. Whenever there is doubt, the natural tendency is toward the status quo. We give up our power to think creatively for the illusion of fearing less, and that default setting needs to change.

That's why I'm so drawn to creativity and a growth mindset. Creativity is rooted in a desire to learn.[3] It embraces challenges, persists despite obstacles, thinks of effort as a means to mastery, and welcomes the chance to learn from criticism.

Trading the status quo depends on tapping creativity. As an agent, I worked in various fields, such as baseball, golf, basketball, and broadcasting, with athletes and coaches. I tapped my creativity to see new ways to expand traditional deals so my clients and their sponsors would benefit. For instance, a golfer who wins on the PGA Tour traditionally gets bonuses from the manufacturers that sponsor that player because their logos are displayed prominently in victory coverage. That doesn't take into account the wall-to-wall coverage of athletes who are playing well, even if they don't win. A player who is leading alone at the end of the first day will own that day's coverage, and certain media platforms are particularly coveted by sponsors. I began to structure sponsorships to include bonuses for appearances on the USAToday.com, *Sports Illustrated* (SI.com), and pgatour.com home pages.

That creative thinking resulted in better contracts for my clients. And my dad's creative thinking helped keep me safe. He showed me the power of bucking the status quo and thinking for myself. I didn't have to solve problems the way other people did. I could try my own way and maybe find it was a better way. He modeled new approaches to problem solving, and that's the mindset I took into my work as a sports agent. That freedom from fear of failure was one of the greatest gifts he's ever given me.

Think of a basic task such as trying to connect with people who are important to your work. Is the best way to contact them in person? Text? LinkedIn? A handwritten note? An assistant or third party? Is there a better time of day? When you see all of these avenues as solutions, you begin to see that every challenge has multiple creative approaches.

A mindset is like software: it runs on a script. If you want to change your performance, you have to change the script running inside your head. You need to replace the words that say, "You either have it or you don't." The creativity script says, "You have the ability to make yourself into anything you want. Your inborn talent is important, but how much you work is even more important. If you can imagine it, you can do it."

By replacing the status quo that holds you back, your creativity will clear a new path apart from others' expectations or your old ones. You effectively are issuing a challenge to yourself to do the work only you can do—using your unique talents, one small decision at a time.

Trade Perfection for Advancement

As kids, we learn to color within the lines. We learn standards and grades. We measure ourselves by statistics, especially if we play sports. We learn to strive for the 100 percent.

Where would we be if we didn't set perfection as a standard for our performance?

Answer: more fearless.

For starters, we often fear less when we let go of perfection. It takes off a ton of pressure when we stop trying to hit such a small mark. And strategically, it makes sense.

Listen to successful people who recognize the shackles that perfection puts on us: "The fastest way to break the cycle of perfectionism . . . is to give up the idea of doing it perfectly—indeed to embrace uncertainty and imperfection," said *Huffington Post* and Thrive Global founder Arianna Huffington.

Her quote points to the importance of paying attention to the small moments of perfectionism that can effectively sabotage career advancement and happiness. Striving for perfection

can get in the way of long-term fulfillment and recognition because we use the expectation of perfection against ourselves.
When we disqualify ourselves because we are not perfect, we
pass up opportunities for growth and advancement.

Consider a research study published in *Harvard Business
Review* that found different outcomes for a diverse group of
job seekers.[4] Men are more likely to feel confident about their
chances when they meet 60 percent of the criteria for a job,
whereas women feel confident only if they can meet all the criteria. Take gender out of it, and this much is true: when we insist
on coloring completely within the lines, we take ourselves out
of the running for jobs that end up going to less qualified competitors. We fear being seen as less than 100 percent ready for
a job. In truth, if you are 100 percent equipped for a job, you
are really qualified for an even better one. So you can see the
multiplier effect of this thinking over time and a significant reason why trading away perfection can help you rise higher more
quickly.

Trading perfection for advancement requires a profound
shift in thinking. It involves reconsidering the small moments
in which perfectionism pulls you into thinking that you are not
good enough, that you have to do more, that you exist in an ei-
ther/or world. You don't.

This trade means giving up what you think you know and
acknowledging the unwritten possibilities that exist. When you
begin to admit, "I don't know what I don't know," you open yourself to curiosity. Instead of, "I can't," you begin to say, "What if?"

This shift is powerful, and I see men and women who don't
do it miss out on chances to stretch and prove themselves, to
sharpen their fearlessness. The researchers described the women
who shied away from jobs in which they lacked 100 percent of
the written requirements this way:

[They] didn't see the hiring process as one where advocacy, relationships, or a creative approach to framing one's expertise could overcome not having the skills and experiences outlined in the job qualifications. What held them back from applying was not a mistaken perception about themselves, but a mistaken perception about the hiring process. This is critical because it suggests that . . . women don't need to try and find that elusive quality "confidence." They just need better information about how hiring processes really work.

When I became president of client representation, I had maybe 25 percent of the qualifications I needed. I had started recruiting talent and building our roster of clients. I had negotiated $50,000 deals, not $50 million deals—yet. I had started to pave the way, but there was still a heck of a gap in my skill set. But there was no gap in my mindset and determination. I felt confident that I could build on the skills I had to meet the great need that I had observed in our company's services. My confidence persuaded the company owner to give me the job.

If I had held on to perfectionism, my career as a sports agent could not have happened. I had to accept that I was far from the perfect candidate, and I had to work my butt off to earn my position. To become president of the firm, I had to let go of perfectionism. This is a key step to fearlessness.

When you see biographies with unusual jumps in positions or career switches, those people are likely to have traded perfection for advancement. They are less worried about what people think than they are worried about how to plug in where they can best flourish.

When you trade perfection for advancement, you become more aggressive about seeing what else is possible. As you do this in the small moments, you are taking on the hard work of changing your default setting to fearing less. You are freeing up the mental space that was on lock down from your perfectionism. Get ready for a big outcome!

Trade Mediocrity for Possibility

What are you OK with?

And is that truly OK with you?

I remember walking into the house where I grew up, excited about the A minus I had scored in a tough class. It was the second-highest score in the class. Most everyone else got Bs and Cs. I was jacked.

My parents wanted all of their children to succeed, of course. So as I showed them my grade and how proud I was, my parents asked me, "Did anyone get an A?"

"Adam did," I said, naming a super smart classmate.

"Hmm. Why did he get the A?"

I felt deflated. That wasn't the response I wanted or expected. But I came to expect that, because part of my parents' approach to encouraging success was reframing my default settings about what my best was.

Perfection wasn't what they were after. It was my potential. It wasn't that I should get an A but that it's worth asking if I could.

They knew I had been comparing down, where all but one of my classmates were. When I bounded into my house, I was happy with that view.

My parents always compared up, never down. They were saying, in two simple questions: How about looking at this small moment differently?

We have the opportunity to help reprogram the way that our team members think. Simply ask: "Are we settling for less than we can achieve?"

Be aware of how you are measuring what is possible, and be careful to stay anchored to your values.

As I was building my career, I remember telling Mom how amazing Michigan State men's basketball coach Tom Izzo was because he was always on. Izzo seemed to be everywhere, in front of high-powered people, the epitome of success in our community. I admired him.

Mom didn't miss a beat. "Molly, you may be right. But Tom Izzo doesn't pack his kid's lunch or schedule teacher conferences. He isn't making dinner. In fact, he probably isn't home for dinner much."

A small moment when I said to myself, "Don't compare yourself to him."

And she was right. Comparing yourself to the wrong people is not good, no matter how wonderful they are. Mom was reminding me of the small moments that grounded me as a kid that I wanted to give my kids as well.

When we chase what is possible simply because someone else has it, we are allowing someone else to define success for us. We are chasing an illusion, a mediocre version of our own potential. We are confusing achievement with fulfillment.[5]

In this scenario, we can't help but open the door to fear. It's scary thinking of trying to live up to someone else's ideals.

Trading mediocrity for possibility highlights the delicate line we walk as individuals, especially as leaders or parents whose responses can carry so much weight. We want to celebrate and, at the same time, point out untapped potential. It's not OK to settle for less because there is almost always more in us that can be applied to our greatest purpose.

On that day of the A minus, I wasn't sensing any fear. I knew my parents had my back and wanted the best for me. As I became independent, I began to see how easy it is for fear to keep us from comparing up.

We can be afraid of taking the lead because it's more comfortable out of the spotlight. We can fear the work that is needed to be number one.

We can fear success because we are used to our current state. It's familiar. No wonder people say, "Be careful what you wish for." Getting what you really want in life can be scary.

When we trade mediocrity for possibility, we aren't deleting our fear. We are facing it and saying we're going to try for our best. When we make that choice of possibility over and over in the small moments, we fear less and set ourselves up for big outcomes. These are possible only when we give up the comfort of mediocrity.

Trade Worry for Compassion

Fear often takes the form of worry. It's the constant drip in your head that distracts us from what we need to focus on. It bleeds energy a millisecond at a time, especially when the object of worry is nothing that we can affect. Worry steals our small moments, and the big outcome of that is lost time and progress.

There's got to be a way to rethink worry, right? Yes, and when we claim it, we can access courage that we didn't think we had. We can get through those moments when we are not in control.

One great antidote for worry is compassion, and here's a family story that helped me understand how powerful this trade can be.

My twin brothers are both pilots. Johnny was a Navy pilot who went through Top Gun school. One of the most dangerous and most important tests of the training is when a pilot has to land the fighter jet on an aircraft carrier.[6] Because the carrier is so big and moves forward, side to side, and up and down, landing the jet has been compared to landing on top of a five-story building during an earthquake.

When the plane lands on the carrier, it goes from about 150 miles per hour to zero in seconds, stopping by catching a hook on a steel wire connected to motors underneath the flight deck. The margin for error can be as little as one foot. They call this "catching the hook."

"It's like trying to land a bulldozer on a postage stamp that's moving around," Johnny told us.

Talk about worried. That was my mom. As Johnny's attempt to catch the hook came closer and Mom's worrying increased, she tapped into her big heart. A giving person who had poured herself into all kinds of community boards, she had seen small moments of generosity lead to big outcomes.

Payday had come, so she had money to go grocery shopping, with Johnny on her mind.

"I knew he had prepared well and that I didn't need to worry, but it was still hard because I knew this was going to be his first time landing on the carrier," Mom told me later. "At the grocery store, I saw a woman and her children with a cart full of groceries, and I could tell she might need help. So I bought them for her."

"It might seem crazy," Mom said. "But I really hoped that by doing that for her, I was sending good fortune to Johnny."

Her logic may not make sense to you, but the point I'm making is that the small moment in the grocery store reflected my mom's mindset. She grasped an opportunity to trade her worry for something bigger.

Many people call this "karma" or "fate." Maybe it's the universe responding to acts of compassion. What Mom did in the grocery store came out of her understanding that wherever you are in life, life gives you many small ways to make a difference.

Johnny's diligence over so many small high-adrenaline moments in his fighter jet paid off. He graduated number one in his class at Miramar (the Navy's Top Gun school), and on that first aircraft carrier landing, he nailed it. Mom lived through it too.

As an agent, I tried to provide a safe space for my clients to move from worry to compassion. When Hall of Fame pitcher John Smoltz was going through a divorce, he often came by my office to sit and talk it through. I understood the pressure he was under as his next pitching appearance loomed. During these times I saw how important vulnerability is to moving away from worry, which so often keeps your heart locked.

I kept an open door for my clients, and I listened and encouraged them to move away from worry because there was nothing good that would come of staying in that place.

Small things can inspire others. You don't have to be Bill Gates writing a big check or taking a big action to change the world. Reinventing your perspective from one of worry to one of compassion happens over time and builds a powerful mindset.

Trade Magical Thinking for Sensible Advice

Someday I will . . .
When I am . . .
If I ever . . .

Do you begin sentences like that? You might be a magical thinker, and if you are, you have a lot of company!

Magical thinking is the perspective that something outside yourself will one day swoop in and create your better life. Someone or an event, even sheer luck, will transform your circumstances. Just like the fairy tale about Jack and the magic beanstalk, magical thinkers are counting on some modern fairy dust to make their dreams into reality.

Fear keeps people thinking this way. It's much, much easier to fantasize about winning the lottery or getting a phone call out of the blue from a recruiter who wants to hand you a dream job on a silver platter.

Even though the magical thinker knows deep down that the mystical ship is not coming in, the fantasizing helps keep the mind busy. This perspective hides fear by dreaming the moments away. Do it enough and you might even fool yourself that you're actively pursuing your personal mission.

But you're not getting anywhere with magical thinking. When fear takes hold, magical thinking leaves you with no grounding. It creates a vacuum.

A small moment early in my career as a sports agent taught me the power of trading magical thinking for sensible advice.

As you can tell by now, I have no problem asking for advice. But when I was starting out, on some level I feared that if I didn't look hard enough and push myself to keep asking, I might not reach the wise person who could change my world view and show me the right way.

I did find him. His name was David Falk. You might have heard of him. He was Michael Jordan's agent. His stable of stars was a who's who of the NBA.

The respect in my eyes worked in my favor with Falk. Ego is almost everything in this world, along with the ability to read people.

I felt confident asking him, and I was aggressive. I was sure I was going to kill it in this field. However, ambition like this is nothing more than magical thinking if it's not grounded in facts and action. That's why I sought Falk's insight.

"You are a legend," I said. "Give me some tips!"

Falk didn't miss a beat.

"Never sign anyone you think will fire you," he replied.

Huh? I scratched my head. I hadn't even considered the end of a business relationship because I was so focused on the start.

Falk's sensible advice spoke to the fear that we often accept without thinking. As we move toward our true purpose, our positive momentum will attract partners and offers. Some are so attractive that magical thinking can take over, making us blind to what else we are accepting.

We see the stars and ignore the sensible advice, and before long we are working with a major client and the fear of getting fired is hanging over our head.

Falk's advice became abundantly clear to me as my career took off and I had the chance to sign and work with great talent. His words helped me get clear on why I was working with someone and what I could see unfolding.

His sensible advice took my head out of the clouds and put my feet on the ground. I recalled his advice in many small moments when I needed courage to trust myself and live with a decision that was right for me. When you decide not to sign someone who will fire you, you're practicing trusting yourself. And that trust drives out fear.

Later, I learned that Falk grew up working in his dad's butcher shop. His dad took his business earnings and chased the magical pot of gold promised by gambling. "My dad was a compulsive gambler who lost everything he had," Falk says.

"My dad was a fun guy. But he was irresponsible. He didn't do the things a man should do to take care of his family."[7]

It makes sense that Falk built his success on loyalty. It's one reason he crafted long-term contracts for Jordan. "He's incredibly loyal, and he'll fight to the death for his clients," Jordan has said.[8]

In the small moments, when we practice trading magical thinking for practical advice, we make ourselves fearless.

8

REPROGRAMMING YOUR DEFAULT SETTINGS

Do one thing every day that scares you.
—Eleanor Roosevelt

Some habits are so natural to us that we do not even recognize them as something we can change. But to fear less, you must take a serious inventory of your patterns of thinking and acting in the small moments of life. Fearlessness becomes fundamental and second nature to us when we reprogram these default settings.

The trades in this chapter create behavioral changes that are particularly important if you want to break out of your current situation. Magical thinking says that you can white-knuckle your way past fear to a new mindset, but in truth, we change our way of thinking about ourselves one small moment at a time. It is not a sudden movement from white to black but rather a gradual movement through gray—from fear, to fearing less, to fearless living.

Change doesn't happen overnight. A drip of actions and decisions brought us to where we are today, and now that stream needs to be diverted in a new, more positive direction. Here are steps that will instill greater fearlessness by resetting your typical reactions.

Trade Agreement for Authority

Saying yes is one of the easiest things we do, and many of us do it without thinking. That's why I think of agreement as one of our default settings.

We say yes without intentionality or a closer look at our values. We say yes because others expect us to say yes. This automatic passivity imposes a huge cost in time and energy. Saying yes because it can be hard and even scary to say no is abdicating control of our life to others.

When we break that cycle, we move toward greater authority and power. Yes, some of us are afraid of actually taking responsibility for our decisions; that's where the automatic yeses often come from. I really encourage you to take an inventory of all the times you agree by default because even if you decide to continue to say yes automatically, you've become more intentional about your small moments, and that's a good step toward awareness.

Let me take you to a place where agreement is often demonstrated. It's any boutique with decent customer service. (I say "decent" because this trade is at the heart of turning decent into great.)

Say you're trying on an outfit. You've entered into a delicate triangle between what you feel you look like, what the mirror says, and what the sales clerk thinks. I used to think that there was nothing better than a clerk who told me I looked great. That's what I thought I wanted to hear. Then I discovered how valuable it was for a clerk to push back. "That one doesn't help you, and here's why" is a good way to establish authority and trust.

Saying no can be hard. What I am suggesting is that sprinkling nos in with your yeses will create greater trust with the people closest to you. Yes all the time is the answer from a doormat. A thoughtful no establishes a boundary of who you are, what you are good at (and not), what you want and don't want. Your default setting doesn't have to be yes!

As a sports agent, I gained confidence with this mindset. I saw how agreement would get me in trouble because it was at odds with my desire for authenticity. It put me in the position of promising more than I could deliver. If there was a place I could add value to a client, I would. There were prospects I tried to recruit whose agents were doing a really great job, and I had to admit, "Gosh, you've got a good agent on your side."

I competed against sports agents who were willing to compromise their relationships with teams and clients on a regular basis. I was not.

We would get our clients' market value, definitely, but we would do all we could not to compromise relationships. I promised that my client service would be more personal and attentive and that they would be happy in a way that they probably had not imagined. People who have stayed only in a Holiday Inn have no idea what the Ritz-Carlton is like. That was where my niche was, and my confidence and authority.

By exercising authority over agreement, I feared less and believed in myself more. My clients and prospects understood that I was a full-service agent who believed in really connecting with them, who was curious about how to make their worlds better. I wanted to make sure their families were taken care of when a trade happened, that they were not overloaded with off-the-field obligations, and that we prepared them for their post-career.

I would tell them that 10 percent of what I did was negotiating their contracts; the other 90 percent was managing their careers. "But my commitment to you," I would say, "is that I'll be one of the few people in your life that you can count on to tell you the truth and not kiss your ass."

This mindset might seem scary if you are used to saying yes. Saying yes is what we think others want to hear, and only after the fact do we realize the true cost of consent.

No is one little word that can bring health, abundance, and happiness. It is a word that sets a boundary between who you are and who others want you to be.

Be careful when saying yes, and don't forget to consider no for its power to build authority. It will also affirm your potential. *No* is an expression of faith that protects your time, talent, and resources for your highest purpose.

You may need permission to say no. So here it is. Try it. Start in the small moments. Trading agreement for authority is a path to fearlessness.

Trade Avoidance for Straight Talk

Very few of us relish tough conversations. We'd much rather avoid confrontation. In fact, our default setting is "Don't rock the boat." We think we are escaping tension this way, but that's just fear talking. To fear less, we need to identify those small moments of avoidance and replace them by embracing straight talk. That's where growth is.

Is there any tougher conversation than a breakup? No one wants to go there, but that's exactly what straight talk is about. The breakup that taught me the importance of this trade wasn't a romantic split. It was an athletic one, and I learned from what I failed to do.

From 13 to 16, I had a great coach, but I didn't think she could take me or my game much further. At age 16, I wondered if maybe I was getting a little stagnant. Did I need new energy and insights? I wanted to take it to another level, and I didn't think my coach had what I needed. She had become robotic in her workouts with me—too routine.

A couple of other good players were working with a different coach. The thought of scheduling a private lesson with him filled me with fear. And guilt that I was doing something really wrong. I felt really bad. I was overwhelmed, worried about how I would do with the new coach and worried about how my current coach would feel if I went to the new coach. I didn't want my current coach to think I wasn't grateful. I simply wasn't mature enough to deal with the situation, so I avoided it.

Eventually I just switched coaches without saying much at all to my former coach. I told myself it was the right decision, and in terms of my tennis game, it was. The new coach changed some aspects of my game and positioned me well to play on a Division I college team.

But I still saw my old coach all the time at the tennis facility. We were still friendly, and we remain connected today. She probably understood on some level that very few teenagers would have had the conversation I regret not having with her.

If I could turn back time, I would have leaned into the discomfort and said what needed to be said: "I can't thank you enough for all you have done for me, but I believe [the new coach] can take me to the next level. It's a more competitive program, and this is the right move for me."

Pushing through the conflict leads to understanding. What I missed out on with my old tennis coach was closure and a chance to become more mature. In retrospect, I know now that I could have chosen to have an honest and frank conversation with her. My default did not have to be avoidance.

This understanding helped me build trust with my clients. I would hear from one of my PGA Tour golfers who was pretty far down on the money list that he had just played a practice round with a guy who was ranked in the top 25. My client would tell me about the 600 grand this other guy was making off the course with endorsement deals, and exclusive outings and so on. I would listen, and I knew what he wanted to hear from me. I could avoid straight talk, but instead I embraced it.

"You're right," I would say gently. "And he is tenth on the money list, and you are not—yet."

In the short term, it wasn't the answer that my client wanted to hear, but it was the truth delivered with clarity. Straight talk is the truth expressed in the small moments. In the long run, this habit helps people trust you. You're not going to simply tell them what they want to hear. You're going to be honest with them.

Choosing straight talk instead of avoidance is the only path to true clarity in a relationship. In my twenties, I met a guy who seemed perfect for me, and I for him. After six months of dating, we got engaged. I felt sure he was The One. When he proposed, saying yes seemed like the only answer.

I was thrilled for my fiancé to meet my parents and brothers. When we visited at Thanksgiving, my family was excited for me. My mom was looking forward to planning her only daughter's wedding.

But in the context of my family, I noticed things that I hadn't before. My fiancé didn't seem all that comfortable. We were playful, and he was serious. I could see friction brewing.

His interpretation of some of our shared values wasn't in keeping with mine. I blended some old-fashioned traditions with independence. He saw his wife as more dependent on him. We were starting out in a complicated situation; how would it be when we added a mortgage and children to the mix?

Of course, this decision was far more complicated than my tennis coach decision. But I had learned the cost of avoidance. I recognized that tension came from fear of displeasing those close to me. I called my family for support, and they gave it. As hard as that conversation was, I broke off the engagement.

This straight talk with my fiancé ultimately opened other possibilities. Years later I met the man who would become my husband, and I was sure this time. We have both valued simplicity and interdependence as we have created a comfortable home, raised children, and provided mutual support.

When we know who we are, we can program our default settings to react authentically and make the wisest decisions. So what if avoidance is our natural instinct? We can choose straight talk. This trade expresses our truest selves and achieves clarity with those closest to us.

Trade Inertia for Repetition

What do you do when the bottom falls out? When something that is essential to your success, and usually almost effortless for you to accomplish, suddenly becomes uncertain?

For me, that happened when I was a sophomore in college on the tennis court. I completely lost my serve. Talk about fear.

I wondered if it would ever come back. And if it didn't, my tennis career was over.

Nothing was wrong with my arm or body or hand-eye coordination. It was totally mental. My default setting for a successful serve had suddenly gone haywire.

I ended up seeing a sports psychologist, who gave me a key practice drill. I got back on the court and repeated my serve, over and over. Each time, I pretended it was 5-all in the third set. It was do or die in my mind every time I served.

Over and over and over, I practiced my serve. I hated the helplessness that I had been feeling, and I was driven to succeed again. I knew I had to keep moving, and the psychologist had shown me how. With each serve, I refined a small moment in anticipation of a big outcome, and soon the fearlessness that I had rehearsed became my reality. Because I made the mental scenario so pressure packed, my practice became the best rehearsal for the real thing. When my serve started to come back, so did my confidence that I could perform when it was most needed. The psychologist had given me mind games that worked to take me out of my rut.

That repetition helped prepare me for those inevitable moments during a match when my arm would tighten and remind me of my fear that my serve would break down again. I couldn't erase that fear entirely. I could, however, lean into the knowledge that I had already practiced, thousands of times, serving for the entire match.

Repetition of success is what peak performers practice. A great football team is going to put its kicker on the line in a simulated two-second drill against its biggest rival. With the pretend game on the line, if the kicker misses, the entire team has to run laps. That's pressure. The team might do this drill 10 times in a row. That's 10 times the pressure.

The practice of high-pressure simulations is the best prevention against choking. When the real thing happens, you know that you have been there many times before and delivered. When you know that, your default setting is self-confidence, not fear.

Losing my serve led to a series of small moments and big impact. By meeting the sports psychologist, I entered a world that had long fascinated me. The mental side of peak performance had intrigued me ever since my dad, a pharmaceutical sales rep, brought home motivational books such as *Swim with the Sharks: Without Being Eaten Alive* and *Outsell, Outmanage, Outmotivate, and Outnegotiate Your Competition*. He read and listened to authors such as Brian Tracy and Zig Ziglar. That interested me even though I didn't exactly know what I was passionate about beyond tennis.

The sports psychologist helped me see what it meant to personally apply the principles that motivational speakers and authors teach. And when my serve came back even better, I knew that these weren't just words, but truth. When I changed my thinking for the better, my performance improved dramatically. I was a very happy customer who never forgot how special this was. As I pushed myself into even more competitive fields beyond college tennis, I relied on a core belief from these mentors—that everyone is destined to do something really great. Including you.

Don't sell yourself short because you are fearful of risk. Don't remain in mediocrity when you know you can do better. If you are experiencing inertia, break through with mental repetition of success. By practicing peak performance in simulations, you are conditioning your mind to expect success and programming your body to deliver those results. Getting unstuck isn't easy, and it is a goal that may well require you to develop new

rituals that replace inertia with fearlessness. You can do it. Start
with small moments of practice.

Trade Instant Success for Seasoning

In observing phenomenal young athletes, I love how they seem
to lack any fear. It's as if they haven't learned to be afraid yet
or to consider the possibility of failure or what it would take to
change course when their rocket ride to success ends.

What makes some of these phenomenal athletes last while
others burn out? I believe it is strong character that is seasoned
through a range of experiences. Stamina comes from identifying
what you need to perform at your peak and thriving through
the inevitable ups and downs. This is not easy under a bright
spotlight.

Before she played in the 2003 U.S. Women's Open, when an
interviewer asked 13-year-old golfer Michelle Wie about burnout, she replied, "I guess I don't really fear it. I guess if I do get
burned out, I'll go to college, and at least I have a chance to
do something else. I'm not really afraid of it because I don't
think—I don't want golf to be my whole life for like the rest of
my life. I just want to do something else, just like play another
sport, because golf is just another game. If I want to take it to
the highest level, I have to be committed. I don't want to get
burned out, but even if I do, I'll have something else to do."[1]

Fast-forward to 2016. At 26, Wie was battling injuries to
her hip, knee, and ankle, as well as mental obstacles. In her first
nine events of 2016, her best finish was a tie for twenty-fifth
place. "It's more a mental thing with Michelle now rather than
physical," her instructor David Leadbetter said. "She has to

come to terms with what she wants to do, what she wants to achieve, and how she wants to achieve it."[2]

Stories like this show us that commitment to a process is important for long-term success. Although instant success is fantastic at the time, it's important to recognize it as a small moment in terms of long-term success. It is just one chapter in a longer story.

Wie has put it this way: "Those wrong decisions, you have to go through that. No one goes through a perfect life. And especially what I did. Especially what my parents had to go through. It was never really done before. You're kind of experimenting. We were learning along the way."[3]

Don't be afraid to think broadly. Reconsider your heavy focus on winning now for a strategy that will season you for the long haul. When you stretch out your timeline, you eliminate the fear of the future. You are paying attention to what's happening now in the context of where you want to go. When you experience a big outcome early, remember that it is just one moment, and keep your long-term focus.

I'm curious to see how Michelle Wie figures all of this out, especially because she is recognizing the power of fear, especially the fear of imperfection. After an off-season in which she went swimming with sharks, she said, "It's just really cool to put myself into experiences where there's so much fear involved, and I can overcome those fears. And that really helps me when I play golf. You know, be like, 'I overcame that, so I can overcome this.'"[4]

Perspective is part of the balancing act of a successful career. The key word is *balance*. It's knowing what you need to do now mindfully and what you need to do next. The highest achievers know the difference and can stay in the moment. It's a bit like using different lenses on a camera to zoom in and also pan out. Don't get stuck in a view of life in which your goals are out of focus.

We will continue to marvel at young achievers who beat the competition in the early stage of their careers. It seems like they can do no wrong. However, it's a fast trajectory that sometimes ends in a flameout. The best know to build on early brilliance with a long-term strategy.

When we trade instant success for seasoning, we dig into the small moments that contribute to a much greater outcome. We are laying out a process for long-term success that avoids burnout.

When we see ourselves in the process of seasoning, we can view our shortcomings and disappointments from a healthier perspective. We give ourselves the gift of time and the leeway and freedom to keep trying. When we recognize that sooner doesn't always mean better, we have reprogrammed a default setting. We fear less because we know we can keep going at a sustainable pace and embrace long-term growth and success.

Trade Ignorance for Education

When I was a sports agent, outsiders often asked me, "Why are so many athletes broke?" My answer could take a while because I had so many examples I had seen or heard about.

I crossed paths with athletes who had suffered because they had made unsecured loans. They would give people they loved $5,000, $10,000, $50,000, $100,000, or more to buy cars, pay mortgages, or start businesses.

Other athletes followed bad advice. They worked with financial advisors who were dishonest and took advantage of the athletes, who would hand over their money with no knowledge of the fees that might accrue or a clear understanding of their investments.

In our firm, we always had athletes sign documents themselves, witnessed by us or a trusted party. The athletes trusted me, so I was used to their asking, "Molly, where do I sign?" I had to remind them to *read the document first and understand it*. Highly paid performers focused so intensely on their skills that they did not allow much bandwidth for critical thinking—especially when money was involved.

Busy businesspeople sometimes have the same habit. Trading ignorance for trust in a third party is always a bad idea when the ultimate responsibility and outcome is on you.

Few things change the quality of our lives like our relationship with money. It's often easier to sign something and stay ignorant of the financial consequences, which is why changing that pattern is so empowering.

Educating yourself and taking control enables you to live fearlessly. This begins learning what you need to know, especially in the small moments.

"Emotions can drive a person to do the wrong things at the wrong times with their money," my friend Ajay Gupta, the wealth manager for speaker and author Tony Robbins, told me. "Investors who work with a fiduciary, have a financial plan, focus on low-cost liquid funds, and have a disciplined rebalancing strategy are the ones who win at building a retirement nest egg."[5]

We make money choices to express our uncertainty. We invest when we see a stock doing well, which is when it costs more. When there's a correction to an investment fund—and all asset classes will have corrections—we fail to react or rebalance. We don't recognize how we are losing money. (A fee increase of 1 to 3 percent is the difference between a 100-pound jockey and a 300-pound one, Tony Robbins likes to say.)

"Fees and taxes are some of the biggest destroyers of wealth, along with emotional decisions," Gupta said. "The people who are truly wealthy don't do what everyone else is doing. They have their own financial plan for taking the right amount of risk and to manage their spending, and they listen to it." In short, they are educated.

The fear is real, and so is the ignorance. That's why this trade can make such a huge difference.

Money tops the personal anxieties measured by the Chapman University Survey of American Fears in 2015.[6] Running out of money in the future was something that 37.4 percent of Americans considered themselves afraid or very afraid of. More specifically, a Gallup poll showed that we worry most about not having enough for retirement and not being able to pay medical costs in the event of a serious illness or accident.[7]

Worldwide, two out of three adults are financially illiterate.[8] Even among Americans who own a credit card or finance a home, Gallup found that one-third did not correctly answer basic questions about compound interest.

It's not easy. Like athletes with the big game on their minds, we all have deadlines and duties that compete for our attention. That is not an acceptable excuse for ignorance.

Education about finances (and this can apply to other parts of life) "changes people in ways that have nothing to do with money rewards," Gupta said. "It's about making an impact for your health and marriage. Money has such a huge connection to so many life stresses that when you create awareness, you have a greater opportunity for stronger relationships with family members and others, for example."

Educate yourself now. The benefits are lasting.

REINVENTING YOUR PERSPECTIVE

It is never too late to be what you might have been.
—George Eliot

You have learned so far that some of the most common behavioral patterns that keep people stuck in fear are the hardest to change.

We have accepted these over time, maybe seeing them as part of our built-in DNA or personality. Maybe these habits have worked well enough for us in the past, but they need to be left behind for us to go forward to fulfill our personal mission.

It's time to tackle these stubborn intruders and build new patterns of fearlessness. It's time to trade habits that skew your perspective. Take off the old lens through which you look at life and put on a new set that is clear and enables you to focus.

If you have ever had your eyes examined, you know what it's like to get the right lens prescription that will help you see at a longer distance and more crisply close up. That is what a fearless perspective is like.

People talk about perspective like a glass of water. Do we see it as half full? Or half empty? A fearless perspective is not that simple. Fear can be the glass itself. A fearless perspective takes hold when we clearly see that the water—what life gives us, our circumstances—is what we make of it. Our glass—the lens we look through at our lives—gets really cloudy with fear.

The trades in this chapter are further ways to see the small moments of life as opportunities to practice fearlessness and to clarify your view of what you have been given. By practicing these new habits and reinventing your perspective, expect to tap abundant energy! That's another big outcome from this hard work.

Trade Uncertainty for Rehearsal

Uncertainty is a given in life. Rarely will you find your way already mapped out. You have to make it happen for yourself. You have to figure it out. Case in point: when I wanted to become a speaker, there was no handbook for making a move like that.

There was fear. I worried that my message wouldn't resonate and that I wouldn't be able to make a living. I didn't spend a lot of time in that fear, but there were moments when those little voices of doubt whispered to me.

This was my challenge: I had to rehearse the person I wanted to be and rehearse the skills I needed to have. I had to give potential clients both a sense of my content and some evidence that I could do what they needed me to do. I had to have the experience before I got the job.

My loyal, supportive husband, Fred, pitched in. We booked hotel meeting spaces and set up a video camera. He was my stand-in for the giant audiences that I hoped to speak in front of one day.

I practiced over and over, did take after take, pretending I was on a big stage. Fred encouraged me and gave me feedback.

Finally, we got the footage I needed to be able to pitch a potential client. A contact of mine who is a speaker reviewed it and assured me of its quality.

Rehearsal is hard! I learned quickly that the things that had made me a great agent were not necessarily what would make me a great speaker. Being a great speaker requires vulnerability and self-deprecation. That openness and empathy are what really connects with an audience. But vulnerability and self-deprecation are not ideal traits for a great agent. My sports clients trusted me because they were confident I knew what information to dispense at the right time.

Rehearsal involved letting go of what made me good in my old world and claiming the traits that would help me succeed in my new world. Rehearsal was key to reinventing my perspective on myself and the image others had of me too.

The product wasn't just the video. I also had the confidence I gained by rehearsing. As a sports agent, I had seen my athlete clients drill like that to erase any doubt of performing under pressure.

Reinventing ourselves always starts with a desire to do something different. Uncertainty creeps in because we are not doing what we want yet, and we may not have done it before. Uncertainty is helpful in that it identifies the gaps in the journey. It stops helping us when it keeps us from filling those gaps.

Every top athlete has dealt with the familiar feeling of uncertainty at some point in his or her career. For future Hall of Fame quarterback Peyton Manning, that uncertainty was magnified in 2012. Would it make him or break him?

After 14 seasons with the team, the Indianapolis Colts made the tough decision to cut Manning, who had missed the entire 2011 season after undergoing neck surgery. Unsure of his future and facing a potentially career-ending injury, Manning could not hide the uncertainty in his voice as he addressed the media with tears in his eyes.

"I have no idea who wants me, what team wants me, how this process works," he told reporters after the news conference. "I don't know if it's like college recruiting where you go take visits. I mean, this is all so new to me."

Faced with the daunting task of both rehabilitating from his injury and finding a new team to play for, Manning returned to what he always did best: he rehearsed for his next chance.

Manning had always been known throughout the league for his intense preparation, but this was something else. This was rehearsing for his next opportunity—an opportunity that was uncertain at best. Many doubted that he would be able to return to the game, much less to the high level of play he was accustomed to.

Channeling that uncertainty into preparation, Manning held secret workouts with his college coordinator, David Cutcliffe. They worked on the fundamentals with hours of tedious drills. The culmination came on March 3, when Cutcliffe ran Manning through a play-by-play simulation of the Colts, 30-17 win in the 2009 American Football Conference (AFC) Championship Game that Manning had quarterbacked.

To make the simulation feel real, Manning went as far as to fly in former Colts teammates and even the former offensive co-ordinator. Play by play, Manning mimicked his three-touchdown performance, calling plays in the huddle and making reads at the line.

No detail was overlooked during the three-hour workout. Each play was run at full speed from the exact yard line and hash mark as the real game. The receivers ran the same routes, and Manning completed the passes to the same targets. When the script called for the Jets to be on offense, Manning and company

retreated to the sideline and waited for the exact time of posses-
sion to expire on the play clock before retaking the field. They
even scripted a 12-minute break for halftime. The only thing
they didn't have were defenders.[1]

———

MANNING WAS REHEARSING for his next moment, so that if
and when it came about, it would feel familiar. Next time you
feel uncertainty creeping in, trade it for rehearsal.

As we take the small moments to rehearse, that uncertainty
has a chance to dissipate, but it doesn't disappear. We have to let
it go. That was part of my process of watching myself on video.
The natural uncertainty I had about selling myself as a speaker
evaporated as I saw myself become more articulate and resonant, clearer and more comfortable.

That's who I wanted to be, and to fully be that, I had to embrace my new skills fully and let go of my uncertainty.

Souvenirs of fear get in the way of reinventing your perspective. Take a line from the movie *Frozen* and let it go.

Trade Gaps for Vision

When there's a gap that needs to be filled, what happens for
you? Do you see opportunity and potential, or do you get frus-
trated that something important is missing?

If I choose to move toward opportunity, I am moving to fearlessness. If I focus on the gap as a problem, I'm going to make
the situation worse. When we are stuck like that, fear can keep
us in the gap. Fear tells us there's no way to fill the gap, or it's
too hard, or we don't have what it takes.

My career as a sports agent took off when I realized that there was a big gap right in front of me and I began crafting an exciting vision for filling it.

My firm, CSE, had been serving its clients since 1986, with a history of helping NBA coaches with their contracts and marketing.

But a gap existed between where we were and where we could be. A vision tugged at me, that we could create more value for our current clientele while going after new talent.

With three local professional sports teams and multiple colleges and universities nearby, I was confident we could sign more talent. We already had a small but respected group of clients, so we wouldn't be starting from scratch.

Could we make a bigger impact by recruiting new talent and expanding our reach beyond our primary focus of NBA coaches? I viewed that gap as a tremendous opportunity for our agency to grow and expand our services.

At the time of this big vision, I was in my early twenties. I had started with the agency a few years earlier, and I was responsible for helping find new endorsement and appearance opportunities for our current clients. I contemplated the idea for a while before I asked our CEO, "What is our recruiting strategy to sign more talent?"

"Current client referrals," he replied confidently.

Hmmm, I thought. Why not be more aggressive? I put together a plan focused on how we could build our baseball division, and then with the brash fearlessness of a twentysomething, I presented it to the owner of the company.

"Go for it," he told me.

If I could put together a business plan and take on the challenge, he was on board. I think he might have thought, "This is going to be interesting," given my lack of experience in baseball, but he loved my grit and tenacity. He respected my fearlessness.

Atlanta Braves pitcher John Smoltz was one of our current clients, so my vision started with building the baseball division around him and recruiting similar talent. Known for his stamina, loyalty, and faith, Smoltz was exactly the kind of great player and person we wanted to attract.

Atlanta was also a hotbed for baseball talent, and there were a lot of young, up-and-coming players who would soon be in need of representation. My strategy was to recruit more baseball players like Smoltz, provide tailored service and support to each one, and keep looking for gaps.

I made it my goal to get all the top talent out of Georgia and to sign one ballplayer in every clubhouse in the major leagues. That way, I had an entry point with every team. I'd ask the players I represented for introductions to anyone they knew had a gap in his support system. We went from representing Smoltz to representing top round draft picks and dozens of big league guys.

We also wanted to do more for our clients beyond the length of their pro sports career. Even before Smoltz retired, we got him into the television booth to give him a taste for broadcasting. Often, athletes who retire want to stay around their sports, and we took care of that gap for them. We told them that we wanted to represent them for life and that we would take care of the small moments so they would have a big outcome.

The other gap that existed was diversifying our client list into other sports. With the goal of expanding into the college coaching space, I recruited and signed Georgia Tech men's basketball coach Paul Hewitt. He took his team to the Final Four, and that created an opportunity for us to renegotiate his contract; that deal caught the attention of other coaches.

My eyes quickly shifted to Tom Izzo, who had built my alma mater, Michigan State, into a basketball powerhouse. We did more for coaches and other clients by offering innovative marketing, public relations, brand positioning, and post-career planning. We had all of those services under one roof. With Izzo signed, we were able to quickly expand our coaches division.

I built our golf division similarly, signing Franklin Langham as our first key client. Langham was a solid PGA Tour pro who liked that we were based in his home state of Georgia. He also liked the way we structured our contracts, which was, basically, if you weren't happy with us, fire us. Most agents in the golf space at the time were locking in players to multi-year agreements. The next year, he finished in the top 25 on the money list and played in the Masters. Langham helped me understand the business side of golf and the gaps he and his peers faced. Through him, we connected with other players, which eventually culminated in our signing Matt Kuchar as our top-tier guy.

We were doing more than expected, signing deals with Fortune 500 firms that had never sponsored PGA Tour golfers or pro athletes of any kind. By then I had been promoted to president of the client representation division of the firm, and I had hired a team of young agents to support each of the divisions.

Trading gaps for vision was everything in the sports agent space. In a field in which there are more agents than athletes to represent, we made our living by identifying and exposing gaps while presenting a vision of possibility. To be successful, we had to be able say to our clients, "These are your current gaps. This is the vision we have for you."

A gap signals to me that *less* is being done than could be. Vision challenges me with the idea of *more*. Is there something that I can do to fill the gap? Could I even exceed that and create an abundance? When you get in the groove of this trade, you will start finding gaps happily because they signal that you have a chance to make a difference.

The only way you fill gaps, I am convinced, is with vision. In the small moments in which we take a step forward, we have to remind ourselves of what we see for ourselves. We haven't achieved it before, so it exists only in our minds.

With each small step forward, as you see gaps, don't get stuck. Reinvent your perspective by returning over and over to your vision. You will unleash incredible energy that suffocates fear and makes it possible for you to fulfill your highest purpose—no matter how many or how wide the gaps.

Trade Obstacles for Assets

Fear presents itself in the obstacles blocking the path to achieving your purpose in life. But those obstacles can be amazing assets too.

Innovative companies such as Apple, Facebook, and Uber confronted the major obstacle of conventional wisdom ("It's never been done like that"), and they disrupted the comfortable status quo. By showing that "it can be done like that," their brands defined innovation. Taking on the critics is a great way to build fearlessness as part of your brand.

On a personal level, obstacles can be anything that is between you and fulfilling your purpose. Is it a lack of money? Not sure of your talent? No support from others?

Face it: those obstacles are worth fearing! Now that we have that out of the way, let's look at how to reinvent your perspective. What if we take a small moment here, do a 180, and approach those obstacles from the opposite position? Just for kicks, consider whether they actually might be assets.

LACK OF EXPERIENCE and name recognition was the biggest obstacle for me in becoming a keynote speaker. If you had Googled my name at the time, you would have found a woman in New York who was a violinist and a model. Not being a celebrity—could that actually be a good thing?—I mulled over this obstacle often as I watched my professional sports clients. They would make big money as speakers who often told stories off the cuff without a clear applicable takeaway for their audience. Because of their name recognition, they were in high demand. Why would anyone want to hear from someone in the wings like me?

Then I shifted 180 degrees: *Why wouldn't they?*

The people on the front line of sports would get paid to talk about executing in tough moments with the world watching, with expectations of their team, city, and fans weighing heavily. So they would talk about what that was like—what it felt like, maybe a bit about their approach or something insider-y that made the audience feel special.

But so often they could not talk about how or why they succeeded at something few people could replicate. For a superstar, no one else seems to be in the same league. Because their work required them to focus mightily on themselves, they had little capacity for any other perspective. Few of them could see their habits or mindset in an objective way that could be communicated to someone who might benefit from this wisdom.

But I could.

I could see—no, I *had* to see—what set apart the best performers. Identifying that difference was my job. It was what I had to pinpoint and sell to a general manager or owner or whoever was negotiating for the services of my athlete, coach, or broadcaster.

Celebrity status, I realized, would almost get in the way of doing that.

Without name recognition, I could build my business with great content spanning my professional and personal experiences. I knew I had come 180 degrees in my thinking when I realized that I didn't have the obstacle of celebrity. My asset was anonymity.

I was free to give my audiences what only I could give them, without the expectations that celebrities face and the ego to go with it. By providing valuable insights from the world of a sports agent, gathered from the wings of the stage, I could share a unique message. I could tell stories that the stars couldn't tell, and often I could tell them better because my position as a sports agent allowed me a unique viewpoint.

When I looked at it this way, I saw what I had to work with as unparalleled.

As I reinvented my perspective, I realized that my experiences were truly singular *because* of the roles I played, not in spite of them. I could talk about nursing a baby and driving to the Masters golf tournament to see my clients. I could talk firsthand about the mindset, discipline, recovery, and resiliency of the elite performers in the world of sports. I could talk about being in a business in which there are more agents than there are athletes to rep and being the only one in the room who's a female. I could talk about negotiating multi-million-dollar deals and raising three kids all born within 12 and a half months.

So much of our fear comes from comparing ourselves to others. Instead, ask different questions and see if the obstacles go away or turn into assets:

- "What can I do that someone else can't?"
- "What do I have that no one else has?"
- "How do I solve a problem in a way that is unique?"

What these questions drill down to is the most important one for reinvention:

- "What perspective gives me the greatest chance of fulfilling my mission?"

Obstacles are real, but they don't need to keep you from reinventing your perspective. In small moments when you see a common roadblock in your journey, do a 180. Try looking at it as an asset.

Claim your journey as your own and no one else's and build habits that move you to greater fearlessness.

Trade Technique for Belief

Talk about scary. For professional golfers, it doesn't get any tenser than what Bubba Watson faced in a sudden death playoff for the 2012 Masters.

His ball was on pine straw under a tree, with tree limbs blocking the shortest path to his target. Everything in the situation said he needed a miracle shot to even have a chance at continuing the playoff.

A poor shot, even an embarrassing one, could be forgiven. It was that difficult. And Watson had never been in this situation because he had never won a major title.

Countless times, every player who competes at the highest level of golf has practiced basic shots with the same club to achieve the same distance. When they have that down, they increase their technique by rehearsing rescue shots from slightly different distances, different terrain, challenging themselves to curve the ball right and left, high and low. These are all the small moments that had shaped Watson's technique.

Here's what it took for Watson to hook a gap wedge 160 yards onto the green. To pull off that miracle, Watson stifled fear by making this trade: he drew confidence not from his physical training but from his mental preparation.

"Belief is more important than technique," he said later in recounting the shot that had won his first green jacket and that had instantly become one of the most memorable moments in golf history.[2]

As Watson sized up the shot, instead of focusing on fear the way 99 percent of golfers would, he examined what he knew and what he had seen.

"One thing about Augusta—we've seen shot after shot out of the trees," Watson said, recalling incredible moments delivered by Phil Mickelson and Tiger Woods, both multiple Masters winners. Watson had not won his first major title yet, but he believed he belonged in their league.

"That was a big thing for me, knowing that it had been done," he said. "When I stood over that ball, I wasn't thinking about the crowd. I wasn't thinking about winning. . . . I got into that zone where everything went blank."

In the pursuit of excellence—in sports, music, business, anything really—there is a similar trajectory. We start out mastering hard skills, the basic hitting or shooting or defending that athletes drill over and over. The scales that musicians rehearse again and again. The fundamentals of finance, accounting, and forming a business plan that a business student or entrepreneur nails and nails again.

Technique is the cumulative result of all those small moments. The more automatic those skills are, the more poised we are to create a big outcome. Often that hinges on our ability to improvise, as Watson did, in the pressurized moment. To face fear through belief.

Watson's success demonstrates the immense value of reinventing our perspective by trading technique for belief. This perspective is what separates the good from the best.

This trade can be just as effective for managers, team members, even parents. At some point you have to step back from critiquing someone's technique. Unless you are a micromanager, you have to stop thinking they could or should do it better and let them do it their way, knowing that you believe wholeheartedly in their abilities. In fact, it may be easier for you to demonstrate belief in others than to believe in yourself.

Whether you are talking to yourself, your team, your entire company, or your family, "I believe in you" is an incredibly powerful statement. It is an expression of faith and hope; it is a statement of fearlessness. In a small moment, it can make a big difference.

———

MY CHILDHOOD HOME had two big hills in the front yard and backyard. I would mow the lawn with a push mower. Dad would tell me to do just the backyard, but if I was done and felt pretty good, he would tell me I had it in me to keep going. Dad wasn't taking my vital signs to make sure I had enough electrolytes to finish the job. He cared about safety, but he didn't judge every little move I was making. He simply believed in my abilities. And that showed me how to believe in myself. His belief in me also taught me the value of persistence and the satisfaction of extra effort in a job well done. I see now that to believe, he had to mentally "leave." He had to let go and trust I could and would handle the big job. And I did.

Is your perspective framed by fear? Or belief? That's what will separate you from others who have achieved your level of technique, who offer the same service or product.

As Watson said, in the moment when you most need it, belief—more than technique—will carry you past fear and vault you above the competition.

Trade Exposure for Innovation

Coaches are an interesting study in fear.

They are judged by one thing above all else, and that is whether they win (I only wish more value were placed on character building of the athletes). With that much pressure, one natural response is to fear losing, to fear failure. You don't have to be a coach to relate to that.

Coaching is a zero-sum game. When coaches win a lot, people expect them to keep winning. When they don't win, people expect them to start winning. Which is an impossible scenario in sports because not everyone can win. Coaches don't directly influence the score. They can put their teams in the position to succeed, but they aren't the ones executing their strategy. The coaches never shoot a three-pointer, throw a curve ball, or make a crucial putt to win. They are on the sidelines.

Competition exposes a coach to so much public judgment. The scoreboard tracks the coach's job performance, summing it up in a game score, season record, and lifetime win-loss tally.

The higher a coach goes, the more the pressure builds. Expectations rise, and in some rabid football programs, for instance, the coach's every move is criticized and second-guessed in real time through social media.

Not all of us work under such intense exposure, and I believe one way to stay fresh and fearless is through innovation—trying new and different methods to get better.

In observing this pressure cooker with my clients who coached at a high level, I saw how the best thrived despite the vulnerability. They had taught themselves to trade that sense of exposure for innovation. They are *so* focused in the moment that is unfolding in front of them and creatively solving the problems presented by the here and now, that they effectively suffocate fear.

A great coach goes into each game with a fresh mindset, knowing that the score is always tied at zero at the beginning of a game. No matter how successful a great coach has been up to that point, each game feels like the first and only one that matters. They're that focused on what is new and what is next.

Innovation is a term that is almost 500 years old, from the Latin word *innovatus*, which means "to renew or change."[3] *Novus* means "new," so to innovate is to go into the new.

When coaches trade exposure for innovation, they shrug off the pressure to spit out victories. That's just noise.

Exposure is pressure. Innovation is fun. Exposure is about "should." Innovation is about "can."

It's so key that we reinvent our perspective to enjoy what we are doing. Yes, work can be a grind, but there are many small moments in which we can choose innovation over exposure, to think about what we are uniquely capable of doing instead of comparing ourselves to others.

Your big outcome will happen when you consistently copy this habit of great coaches. When you feel exposed, lean in.

Determine to grow through that vulnerability. By reinventing your perspective, you will neutralize that pressure from outside judgment, be in the moment, and stay stimulated in your outlook.

Innovation reminds us that no matter what critics say about our performance, today and this moment are all we have.

10

UNIFYING YOUR TRIBE

What counts in life is not the mere fact that we have lived.
It is what difference we have made to the lives of others
that will determine the significance of the life we lead.
—Nelson Mandela

Your tribe consists of the people whom you depend on and who depend on you. They are involved intrinsically in your biggest outcome. They have the most to benefit from your fearlessness and the most to lose from your fear.

We belong to them and they to us, and if that breaks apart, it weakens both. Fearless generosity, however, leads to unimaginable growth.

Fearlessness is a great unifier, and unifying your tribe is a great stepping-stone to fearing less. When other people have your back and you have theirs, together you can do that *Star Trek* thing of boldly going where no one has gone before. You can be fearless—together.

At the heart of unifying your tribe is adopting an abundance mindset. Instead of thinking that success is a zero-sum game, the abundance mindset believes that what we get from giving is far more than we actually give. The abundance mindset allows us to share with others fearlessly even in the most competitive environments because we are truly connected with our purpose.

Whether you are an introvert, on a work team, or part of a family—and especially if you manage people—it's critical to encourage in others what you also hope for yourself. Nurturing the goal of fearlessness in others will boost your own.

When you unify your tribe, you promote an attitude of "we first" instead of "me first." That guides the small moments of making decisions that build up to a big outcome for your tribe. To help get there, turn the page to the final three trades in this book.

Trade Critics for Cheerleaders

I met Robyn Spizman in 2009 when I spoke to a business group of about 50 people and was still an agent. They were meeting at lunchtime, and the location was right across the street from my office. I had been trying to speak to groups whenever my schedule allowed, so this was a perfect opportunity.

After working with coaches as a young athlete and majoring in communications, I felt in my soul that I had something inspiring and important to say to others, to help them approach life in a more meaningful, holistic way. I had learned so much about working on a tightrope, negotiating high-stakes deals as a sports agent and establishing fearless conversations in which deals could get done. I had thrived as a woman in a male-dominated industry. There were so many lessons I had learned that I wanted to impart to others.

I loved encouraging people, cheering them on to be their best, especially given other people's natural inclination to criticize, to look for the one thing that went wrong. Encouragement was a natural attribute that helped differentiate me as a sports agent, a business colleague, wife, mother, and friend.

With three young kids at home and a busy work pace, I was motivated to practice speaking, but I had not thought much past the points I wanted to make in the lunch speech.

When I finished the talk, Spizman came up to me.

"You need to do this!" she said excitedly.

"What do you mean?" I asked.

"You need to speak! You have a lot to say," she said. "You're really good."

I felt wonderful hearing that feedback. Spizman was well on her way to writing more than 70 books, sharing helpful and practical tips with consumers. She is best known as a gift-giving expert whom you might have seen on the *Today Show* demonstrating thoughtful ways to wrap holiday presents.[1] ("Spreading kindness is the greatest gift we can give one another" is one of Spizman's mottos.)

"I'd love your advice," I told her.

Spizman graciously shared her considerable knowledge of publishing and marketing with me. She advised me on how to collect video content and set up my own website. She guided me through the steps that helped me publish my book *The Business of Being the Best* about the traits of peak performers. Her spirit of generosity and inspiration was invaluable as I transitioned from my job at the firm to starting my own company.

Then another cheerleader came into my life. Chris Johnson had been my fitness trainer when I played college tennis. He had segued into corporate speaking through his company On Target Living, which aims to improve health and performance by focusing on the small steps people can take toward healthy living.[2] We realized there was synergy between his clients and my message, and it was different from his message. "Let me introduce you to a few insurance and financial institutions that are looking for speaking talent," Johnson offered.

A few months later I was booked with both, and we were sharing the same booking agent. Between the marketing advice, referrals, and connections, my purpose was being realized. I was making a far greater impact on many people in my audiences than I could have as a sports agent. I loved what I did in sports, and I was falling even more in love with speaking and entrepreneurship.

The boost from my cheerleaders was priceless. Had I not been open to receiving encouragement, had I gravitated to the critical voices that are in all of our lives, I would never have changed. Naysayers tell us to fear change, to fear what isn't done or what isn't done quite right.

Experience has taught me that we receive far more than we give. As much as I encouraged my professional sports clients to fearlessly confront obstacles and push past those obstacles and bad news, so much more encouragement came back to me. Spizman and Johnson are two examples of cheerleaders who could see more for me because they were in the world that I had not entered yet. They could see my success and made the effort to boost me toward it.

The single most important cheerleader in my quest for fearlessness is my husband, Fred. His humble brilliance and support for me and our daughters is magical. The key word is *support*. Fred, in his actions, defines what genuine support and sacrifice look like, and he inspires me to live up to that standard. He is an all-star father to Emma, Meg, and Kate, and his professional success in commercial real estate and personal passion for helping with homework create a rock-solid foundation for our family.

His leadership, generosity, strong faith, and consistent love make him far more than a cheerleader. He embodies the ideal that whatever you want to see come to you, it's up to you to put out into the world first.

Are you listening to critics or surrounded by them? They are a tribe stuck in fear. Trade for the person you want to be to others. Cheer someone on and you will find someone—perhaps many people!—ready to support you as you pursue fearlessness.

Trade Scorekeeping for Sharing

When Jim Clark was leading the Boys and Girls Clubs of Milwaukee, he met his numbers. The organization was viewed as successful, with a staff and board that worked well to serve the children in the community.

But the metrics weren't telling the whole story, Clark knew, and that bothered him. He believes that when it comes to individuals or groups, no one is standing still. You're either going up or going down.

While the spreadsheet told him his leadership was adequate, his focus was on the need around him.

"It was a small moment that hit me like a lightning bolt," Clark told me. "As good as we are, as hard as we are pushing at our peak, we aren't good enough. The kids we are serving have lived a life of broken promises, and we're not making a big enough impact on this community. How can we have an even more significant impact?"[3]

Clark began to share a new vision that went far beyond the scorekeeping results. The numbers of kids served, locations, and program outcomes helped only as a starting point for where they would go next. In his vision, the organization would nearly triple its capacity in an effort to create a "decade of hope" for needy kids in Milwaukee.

As you might expect, the plan involved an unprecedented level of fund-raising, and many doubters raised their voices. The organization was taking on too much risk, they said. What if the Milwaukee community didn't share the funds and resources it would take to achieve this goal? The vision required so many other stakeholders to buy in. It was a bold move to go way up that could end up pulling them way down. Was it worth it?

"The plan was a shocking thought for people at first," said Clark, who was focused on the generosity and resources that he believed his community could and would share if they could see how much good they could do. "The echo in my head said that we couldn't compromise. That's when a leader has to create the atmosphere and environment in which this can happen."

To inspire his staff to buy into the shared vision, Clark made a commitment to lead no matter what. "Relentless pursuit" became a motto that his staff became used to hearing him use. His vision had numbers and goals, but the numbers and goals were not his vision. To shift the culture, he had moved from *keeping score* of old standards of competency to *sharing* a new vision of possibility and asking the community to share the work of executing it.

By trading the expected way of doing business, Clark created greater unity for his tribe. The staff and volunteers came together to serve the Milwaukee kids; by sharing his inspiration, Clark unified them behind a higher purpose. As they grew and adapted to the vision, their work began to reach more of the children who needed help, and more partners got behind the vision. Sharing led to a great impact in this Wisconsin city.

After eight years as president and CEO, he helped the Milwaukee affiliate become one of the largest and most successful Boys and Girls Clubs in the country. Under his leadership, the organization had seven consecutive years of revenue growth, even in the darkest years of our nation's economic recession, and it added 17 new service locations. Average daily attendance and frequency had increased, and staff had more than doubled. The innovative programs that he had sparked helped increase positive outcomes in high school graduation, teen services, and college preparation.

His lightning bolt moment eventually led to the organization's securing a $4.1 million federal education grant to scale its literacy program. Today the Boys and Girls Clubs of Greater Milwaukee has 700 employees, more than 300 volunteers, and 40 locations.

The most important number: they serve more than 35,000 young people annually. That's a ton of small moments in connection with kids whose lives may depend on someone's reaching out. Almost 60 percent of Boys and Girls Clubs of America (BGCA) alumni across the country say that the BGCA saved their lives, a Harris Poll has reported.[4] The shared vision led to a huge outcome!

Clark's career benefited too. He was promoted to national president of the BGCA, which I serve as a board member. He is charged with unifying the services of more than 4,200 clubs to nearly 4 million young people each year, providing a safe place, caring adult mentors, fun, friendship, and high-impact youth development programs on a daily basis during critical nonschool hours.

On this high-profile platform, Clark continues to share his relentless pursuit of possibility. "We have to be one of the catalysts that drive change," he told the media in Atlanta, where BGCA is headquartered. "We have to do more for kids than ever before."[5]

Clark's experiences reflect the power of trading scorekeeping for sharing. Sharing involves risk. It can be a small moment when we give up our careful to-do list and share our time and effort to help a friend in need.

Sharing may not pay the bills in the short term. It can be difficult to let go of scorekeeping, of measuring success by numbers and quantifiable outcomes, but the results happen when you focus on the vision. When you go above and beyond the way Clark did to tap into a deep vein of sharing, you take a risk to unify your tribe. With fearlessness like this, the universe will go to work for you.

Trade Speculation for Transparency

In the wake of Wall Street's meltdown, small businesses like that of Cynthia Jones Parks were suffering greatly. Jones Worley Communications was struggling to pay its employees, and Parks was dipping into her personal money to ensure that they got paid. She could only speculate on when her clients might be in touch because most of her contracts had been canceled or were awaiting funding. "I didn't know what we were going to do," she recalled.[6] Her tribe was depending on her leadership to survive.

At a critical crossroads like that, we all long to see clearly what we need to do. We crave a concrete plan to reverse the spiral and move toward recovery and success. In the meantime, speculation erodes trust.

One way to build trust is with great transparency. When people know how we do business, they know what to expect.

When they know how our purpose will be executed, trust is built or restored. That's why trading speculation for transparency, especially in the small moments, is so important to unifying your tribe.

A spiritual person, Parks prayed for guidance for many months. One night she bolted awake at the sound of a divine voice telling her that she had already been blessed. "Go do something with it," she heard the voice tell her.

But what was that something? Her company's historic office building came into focus. The empty office furniture and dimmed lights depressed everyone, and the space was long overdue for a makeover. What about now? It would be a bold move to bring light into a ground floor that was so dark, like the company's prospects.

The next day, despite her staff's admonishment that the firm had no money, she borrowed $50,000 on credit. Soon ground broke on the renovation. Yes, there was fear rippling through the firm, but she consciously let it go. When people speculated on her strategy, she responded that she was focused on taking advantage of her blessings. She didn't have anything to hide. Not long after, she invested the same amount to redo the top floor.

The building filled with new light and life. A new studio unified her staff and the community groups and other companies that rented it for meetings and conferences. She hung her paintings on the wall, an acknowledgment of her artistic talent.

Parks fearlessly created a place where teamwork was more possible and more enjoyable. By shining a light on her process, she created transparency with her clients and staff. The renovation was proof of the intention to thrive amid economic uncertainty.

We think of transparency as the way of doing business in our hyperconnected world where so much of what used to be private is now public. Today our tribes expect to know more about what we do, how we do it, and why.

When your actions consistently align with your purpose, your tribe is less likely to speculate or worry, and they are more likely to bond. Loyalty comes when your tribe feels like they really know you, and this transparency can become a strong foundation for individual and collective fearlessness.

Let me offer a specific example as well. On teams that I manage, I try to foster a culture of speaking up for what you need and never speaking down to group members. Recently, I helped my 12-year-old daughter move away from speculation about why her volleyball coach wasn't giving her more playing time and coming up with a strategy to speak up to the coach about her desire to contribute more to the team. "Pick your spot, and I am here to support you," I told my daughter.

As I waited in the car, she approached the coach and asked politely, "What do I need to work on to get more playing time?" The coach told her to work on her serve and be ready to compete because the possibility of her playing was closer than she might have thought.

With that encouragement, my daughter worked tirelessly on her serve and steadily improved. A week later, the coach kept her in the entire game. That was big, but that wasn't all. She continued to contribute, and bench time became rare. By the end of the season, she won Most Valuable Player. I was proud of that honor, but I was even more proud of how she had fought past assumptions to understand clearly what she needed to do to reach her goal.

Normally my daughter is fearless about speaking up at home, and her barriers to speaking up with her coach made me think. How can we at the core of what we are doing attempt to be fearless in all our relationships in an appropriate way? What does that kind of fearlessness look like for me and for the other members of my tribe? I believe transparent communication is essential for creating a no-fear zone for those whose outcomes are linked closely with our own.

Parks's fearlessness led to clarity in her firm's purpose and vision too. She saw that the smart card branding campaign that she had rolled out for Atlanta's mass transit system could be packaged and marketed to other cities.

Over the next few years, she worked on transportation projects in California, Missouri, Pennsylvania, and Florida. Today her clientele includes Fortune 500 corporations, healthcare organizations, educational institutions, nonprofits, and government agencies.

As you and your tribe move from a fear perspective to a fearless mindset, expect to see different levels of push or resistance. Like Parks, we can model fearlessness through our actions or stay stuck in the darkness of fear. We can speak up and give voice to our concerns and speculation. We have so many small moments of opportunity to influence those around us. Will you join me in fearlessly choosing transparency?

CONCLUSION

I t is my greatest hope that this book has inspired you to become aware of behavior patterns that are keeping you stuck in fear and that you can trade those habits for rituals that are aligned with your purpose. It doesn't happen overnight, and hopefully this book will be a guide to a life-changing journey to fearing less.

I hope you will always stay open and tap into your vulnerability. Expect the unexpected. It is so important to maintain a mindset of openness and curiosity. Openness is the wide lens with which you can see in the moment, and it is the knowledge that there is much that you don't know.

Without curiosity, you can't have the awareness that I describe as 360 degrees, the kind of sensitivity that is important in all relationships and behavior. With openness and curiosity, you understand that every action plants a seed for something else to happen, now or in the future.

This conclusion offers you a way to put some of what you have read into action. Here's a spot for you to reflect on what aspects of this book apply most to your life and that you can use

to start planning for more favorable behaviors during the small
moments of opportunity:

My purpose or mission statement:

_____

_____

_____

Fears that are holding me back from living my purpose:

_____

_____

_____

To work on my fear of _____, I will trade
_____ for _____ in anticipation that this behavior
in small moments will result in _____,
which is in line with my purpose. A typical small moment
in which I can practice this trade looks like this:

_____

_____

_____

To work on my fear of _____, I will trade
_____ for _____ in anticipation that this behavior
in small moments will result in _____,
which is in line with my purpose. A typical small moment
in which I can practice this trade looks like this:

_____

_____

_____

To work on my fear of _ _____, I will trade
_____ for _____ in anticipation that this behavior
in small moments will result in _____,
which is in line with my purpose. A typical small moment
in which I can practice this trade looks like this:

_____

_____

_____

    Your journey from fear to fearlessness is important to me, and I hope you will share it with me and with others because fearlessness is contagious. You can reach me directly at molly@ mollyfletcher.com or connect on Twitter, Facebook, LinkedIn, or Instagram. I am grateful for your interest in the approaches I have shared, and I look forward to keeping up our conversation about fearlessness. Your suggestions and feedback are always welcome.

    If you consistently employ the methods that I've described in these pages, you will become more fearless and purposeful. You will recognize the power that exists within the small acts of fearlessness, and this awareness will propel you off the sidelines and into becoming the hero of your journey. You'll pay more attention to the 1,440 minutes that each day offers, and you'll approach these moments as opportunities for intentionality and authenticity.

    Remember, "Small moments, big outcomes." This doesn't happen all at once. Practice your new ways of thinking and acting, and you will begin to see your life change.

    Become fearless, one moment at a time.

NOTES

Introduction

1. http://www.gallup.com/poll/192575/employee-engagement-slips-below-may
   .aspx.
2. http://mindsetonline.com/abouttheauthor/. See also Carol Dweck's powerful
   book *Mindset: The New Psychology of Success*, Ballantine Books, New York,
   2016.
3. http://www.charylstrayed.com/brave_enough_127560.htm.
4. https://www.khanacademy.org/youcanlearnanything.
5. http://www.aafp.org/news/2016-congress-fmx/20160930fmx-levine.html.
6. http://www.cbssports.com/nba/eye-on-basketball/22491792/nba-finals-a
   -rock-a-hammer-and-the-cracking-of-the-spurs-majesty-in-game-7.
7. https://hbr.org/2014/12/what-bosses-gain-by-being-vulnerable.

Chapter 1

1. http://www.penguin.com/ajax/books/excerpt/9780143114345.
2. https://www.macfound.org/fellows/636/.
3. In fact, my blog on curiosity-based leadership is one of the most popular ones
   I have written: https://mollyfletcher.com/curiosity-based-leadership/.
4. https://www.entrepreneur.com/article/197614.
5. http://www.brainyquote.com/quotes/quotes/j/jodiefoste587529.html.
6. Adapted from *The Human Performance Institute*, https://www.jjhpi.com.

7. http://www.ted.com/talks/karen_thompson_walker_what_fear_can_teach_us /transcript?language=en.
8. https://www.amazon.com/Rise-Superman-Decoding-Ultimate-Performance /dp/1477800832/ref=sr_1_1?ie=UTF8&qid=1467501289&sr=8-1&key words=rise+of+superman.
9. https://mollyfletcher.com/personal-mission-statement/.
10. http://www.biography.com/people/dara-torres-20837363.

Chapter 2

1. http://www.foxsports.com/nfl/story/dallas-cowboys-sean-lee-decided-to-pass -on-2m-bonus-010316.
2. http://www.foxsports.com/nfl/story/dallas-cowboys-sean-lee-decided-to-pass -on-2m-bonus-010316.
3. Interview with Carla Harris on June 27, 2016.
4. http://baseballhall.org/hof/class-of-2015.
5. http://diananyad.com/my-invite-to-cuba/.
6. http://www.adweek.com/agencyspy/star-athletes-never-lose-the-love-in-tbwa chiatday-l-a-s-latest-for-gatorade/111246.
7. http://www.sportsonearth.com/article/91281874/to-understand-peyton -manning-one-has-to-know-where-he-came-from.
8. https://www.fastcocreate.com/3054789/behind-the-brand/joy-mangano-rolls -out-her-blueprint-for-your-million-dollar-idea.

Chapter 3

1. http://www.golfdigest.com/story/anatomy-of-a-masters-collapse.
2. http://www.jimmyv.org/about-us/remembering-jim/jimmy-v-espy-awards -speech/.
3. http://www.sportingnews.com/ncaa-basketball/news/jim-valvano-nc-state -jimmy-v-foundation-cancer-research-birthday/ggcgqbgxst931467civf5de68.
4. http://www.dailyinfographic.com/wp-content/uploads/2015/03/Small-Biz -Survey-V2.png.
5. http://www.leapleyconstruction.com/about-us/our-leadership/meredith -leapley/.
6. Interview with Meredith Leapley on April 5, 2016.
7. https://www.amazon.com/Dare-Serve-Superior-Results-Serving/dp /1626562350/ref=sr_1_1?s=books&ie=UTF8&qid=1476238452&sr =1-1&keywords=dare+to+serve.
8. Popeyes Louisiana Kitchen, "Our Story," www.popeyes.com.
9. http://www.bcbsnc.com/livefearless/mia-hamm-live-fearless-story/.

10. http://www.bbc.com/capital/story/20160316-the hidden-psychology-of
    -failure.
11. https://hbr.org/2016/03/your-desire-to-get-things-done-can-undermine-your
    -effectiveness.
12. www.ziglar.com.

Chapter 4

1. https://www.ted.com/talks/david_blaine_how_i_held_my_breath_for_17
   _min.
2. http://www.nasa.gov/feature/nasa-hacks-the-real-stories.
3. https://www.ted.com/talks/mihaly_csikszentmihalyi_on_flow/transcript?
   language=en.
4. https://www.amazon.com/Rise-Superman-Decoding-Ultimate-Performance
   /dp/1477800832/ref=sr_1_1?ie=UTF8&qid=1467501289&sr=8-1&
   keywords=rise+of+superman.
5. http://gregmckeown.com/essentialism-the-disciplined-pursuit-of-less/.
6. Ibid.

Chapter 5

1. See my blog on mollyfletcher.com on this topic for more examples.
2. http://www.espn.com/nba/playoffs/2012/story/_/id/8080433/lebron-james
   -read-nba-finals.
3. See www.tommynewberry.com.
4. https://www.amazon.com/Rise-Superman-Decoding Ultimate Performance
   /dp/1477800832/ref=sr_1_1?ie=UTF8&qid=1467501289&sr=8-1&
   keywords=rise+of+superman.
5. From *The New Writer's Handbook 2007: A Practical Anthology of Best Advice
   for Your Craft and Career*, https://www.amazon.com/New-Writers-Handbook
   -2007-Practical/dp/0976520168.
6. http://www.huffingtonpost.com/entry/social-media-anxiety_us
   _56534766e4b0d4093a587400.
7. http://www.nytimes.com/2016/05/06/business/facebook-bends-the-rules-of
   -audience-engagement-to-its-advantage.html?_r=0.
8. You can read more about this strategy on my blog in an article called "Embracing the Power of Pause," mollyfletcher.com.
9. https://www.usagym.org/pages/home/publications/technique/1996/10
   /fear.pdf.
10. http://www.americanrhetoric.com/speeches/ewieselperilsofindifference.html.
11. http://m.mlb.com/news/article/5805268//.

12. http://m.mlb.com/news/article/170989452/braves-jeff-francoeur-comes-in -full-circle/.
13. http://www.supersoul.tv/supersoul-sessions/the-anatomy-of-trust/.
14. http://greatergood.berkeley.edu/article/item/john_gottman_on_trust_and _betrayal.
15. http://www.inc.com/john-boitnott/how-to-avoid-getting-taken-in-by-your -office-gossip.html.

Chapter 6

1. http://www.espn.com/blog/seattle-seahawks/post/_/id/19957/russell -wilsons-commencement-speech-at-wisconsin.
2. https://mollyfletcher.com/gifts-of-rejection/.
3. https://www.youtube.com/watch?v=xPuJ4wcAei8.
4. http://saportareport.com/lee-katzs-grant-field-moment-selling-peanuts-as-a -teenager-taught-him-lasting-lessons-in-deal-making/.
5. https://mollyfletcher.com/takeaways-from-leadercast/.
6. http://news.wisc.edu/russell-wilson-2016-commencement-speech-when-life -tells-you-no/.
7. http://sethgodin.typepad.com/seths_blog/2013/06/fearlessness-is-not-the -same-as-the-absence-of-fear.html.
8. http://www.si.com/mlb/2016/09/01/jeff-francoeur-marlins-braves-career -sports-illustrated.
9. Interview with Pat Miller on June 20, 2016.
10. http://www.airspacemag.com/as-interview/aamps-interview-sullys -tale-53584029/#SV6gMd2IMa39kB0Q.99.

Chapter 7

1. http://www.salary.com/most-people-don-t-negotiate-due-to-fear-lack-of -skills/.
2. Ibid.
3. http://mindsetonline.com/.
4. https://hbr.org/2014/08/why-women-dont-apply-for-jobs-unless-theyre-100 -qualified.
5. https://mollyfletcher.com/difference-achievement-fulfillment/.
6. http://www.popsci.com/blog-network/shipshape/several-reasons-why -aircraft-carriers-are-super-dangerous.
7. http://www.sportsbusinessdaily.com/Journal/Issues/2015/02/23/Champions /Falk.aspx.
8. Ibid.

Chapter 8

1. http://www.asapsports.com/show_interview.php?id=11859.
2. http://www.golfdigest.com/story/david-leadbetter-michelle-wies-problems-more-mental-than-physical.
3. http://www.golf.com/tour-and-news/golf-live-qa-michelle-wie-going-gluten-free-swimming-sharks-and-trying-rediscover-her-childhood-swing.
4. Ibid.
5. http://guptawealthmanagement.com/team-gupta/.
6. https://blogs.chapman.edu/wilkinson/2015/10/13/americas-top-fears-2015/.
7. http://www.gallup.com/businessjournal/190601/consequences-debt-america.aspx?version=print#main.
8. http://www.gallup.com/poll/186680/two-three-adults-worldwide-financially-illiterate.aspx?utm_source=genericbutton&utm_medium=organic&utm_campaign=sharing.

Chapter 9

1. http://www.nola.com/saints/index.ssf/2012/10/post_235.html.
2. http://www.golf.com/tour-and-news/bubba-watson-hook-shot-2012-masters-oral-history.
3. http://www.fastcodesign.com/1663265/what-do-we-mean-by-innovation-collaboration-or-design.

Chapter 10

1. http://www.today.com/video/creative-wrapping-with-wine-socks-egg-cartons-toilet-paper-590051395660.
2. See ontargetliving.com.
3. Interview with Jim Clark on April 22, 2016.
4. http://www.bgca.org/newsevents/PressReleases/Pages/BGCA_TriplePlayMobileTourTravelsToInspireHealthFitness.aspx.
5. http://saportareport.com/jim-clark-takes-helm-at-boys-girls-club-of-america/.
6. https://saportareport.com/cynthia-jones-parks-awoke-to-moment-prompting-her-to-borrow-and-invest-in-middle-of-recession/.

INDEX

ABOUT THE AUTHOR

 **Molly Fletcher** is a trailblazer in every sense of the word—a rare combination of business wisdom, relationship brilliance, and unwavering optimism. As CEO of the Molly Fletcher Company, she shares the unconventional and unique techniques that helped her thrive as one of the first female sports agents in the high-stakes, big-ego world of professional sports and now as a successful entrepreneur.

As president of client representation for the sports and entertainment agency CSE, Fletcher spent two decades as one of the world's few female sports agents. Hailed as the "female Jerry Maguire" by CNN, she recruited and represented hundreds of the biggest names, including Hall of Fame pitcher John Smoltz, PGA Tour golfer Matt Kuchar, broadcaster Erin Andrews, and champion basketball coaches Tom Izzo and Doc Rivers. As she successfully negotiated over $500 million in contracts for her clients and built lasting relationships, she also observed and adopted the traits of those at the top of their game.

Fletcher has been featured on ESPN and in *Fast Company*, *Forbes*, and *Sports Illustrated*. A sought-after motivational speaker, she delivers game-changing messages to top companies, trade associations, and teams worldwide.

She is the author of three other books: *A Winner's Guide to Negotiating*, *The Business of Being the Best*, and *The 5 Best Tools to Find Your Dream Career*.

Among her many accolades, Fletcher is most proud of her Outstanding Alumni Award from Michigan State University, where she earned a bachelor's degree in communications while captaining the women's tennis team. She currently serves as a National Trustee member for the Boys & Girls Clubs of America, and she was a board member of Children's Healthcare of Atlanta.

Fletcher's energy and passion for life shine through in everything she does. She finds her greatest joy at home in Atlanta, Georgia, with her husband, Fred, and their three daughters.

For more information, please visit mollyfletcher.com.